Advance Reader Copy
For Promotional Use Only

World Poetry Books
Pub Date: November 9, 2026

Publicity Contact:
publicity@worldpoetrybooks.com

Ordering and Distribution Info:
worldpoetrybooks.com/orders
orders@worldpoetrybooks.com

Valentine Penrose

Of Thorn and Wing
Collected Poems

translated from French by Mia X. Pérez

introduction by Felicity Gee

WORLD POETRY

First Edition, First Printing, 2026
ISBN 978-1-954218-54-3

World Poetry Books
New York, NY
www.worldpoetrybooks.com

World Poetry titles are distributed by Asterism Books (US) and Turnaround Publisher Services (UK). Subscriptions and standing orders are available from the publisher.

Library of Congress Control Number: 2026948898

Cover design by Clever Hans
Typesetting by Don't Look Now
Printed in Lithuania by BALTO Print

World Poetry Books is a 501(c)(3) nonprofit and charitable organization founded in 2017 in New York City, a member of the Community of Literary Magazines and Presses (CLMP), and a member of the publishing cooperative Poetry Corp. Our publications and programs are made possible by grants from the Poetry Foundation, Hawthornden Foundation, and the New York State Council on the Arts with the support of the Office of the Governor and the New York State Legislature, and supported by an affiliation with the Humanities Institute and the Translation Program at the University of Connecticut (Storrs), as well as individual donors and subscribers. To learn more or to make a donation please visit our website: worldpoetrybooks.com/support.

Table of Contents

Uncollected Poems

Dark Luminescence: Valentine Penrose's Antinomies of Enchantment

Felicity Gee

Valentine Penrose wrote with her heart in her opposite palm, each hand weighing the wonders of the world against its horrors. A dedicated poet from her youth, she was also an avid letter writer, collagist, researcher, and novelist. Her poems are direct yet expansive, deeply personal, and often in passionate communication with a wider humanity. They do not shy from the realities of war and conflict, nor the sufferings of the body and its desires. They offer the reader in the twenty-first century a map to arcane mysteries of the twentieth, a map that operates through a marvelous and heterogeneous index. Such mysteries, often stemming from her fascination with astrology, Tarot, botany, Greek and Roman mythologies, Vedic mysticism, and European history, are untethered from their coordinates of origin. They voice a world language, speaking from a transnational perspective that flows against the colonial and imperial forces of a rapidly shifting Europe. Writing of the potential of wonder as "a considered and strategic act," anthropologist Tulasi Srinivas posits that it can produce "coexistent temporalities and spatialities," encouraging a rethinking of modern existence that acknowledges "differential, and previously distant and invisible perspectives."[1] Valentine Penrose's poems similarly transmute time and space, holding a sense of wonder that eclipses many horrors. If the darkness is not completely extinguished, it is because the poet herself understood that the path to liberty involved philosophical anguish.

In her quest to understand the world's capacity for magic, she refused to fit in, or to stay still, instead eschewing heteronormative ideals of love or family to follow her desires. She loved women above all, and this is reflected in the uniquely Penrosean environments of her poems where sapphic energies are woven together with the spiritual powers at play:

> Featherless on the edge
> skinless on the edge
> my beautifully sheltered sister watched me fall
> and I laughed within her.

The naked, permeable female body provides both inspiration and intimacy, the other so close at hand to the poet as to become one with her. Lilith, Sleeping Beauty, Jean Rhys's Antoinette Cosway (the "Madwoman of Sargassum"),[2] Mary Magdalene, Mother Kali, Countess Erzsébet Báthory, angels, and weird sisters, as well as lovers and versions of mirrored selves, communicate with the reader of these poems, calling her to participate in a metamorphosis. Spells are cast, and a path opens—the title of her collection *Sorts de la lueur* (published in 1937) could be translated as "Glow Spells," or "Spells of the Glimmer." In her 1951 collage-novel, *Dons des féminines* (Gifts of the Feminine)—two protagonists, Rubia and Maria Elona, voyage across vast land and moonscapes, unbound by social constraints or domestic labor. They witness miracles and retreat at night to profound lesbian intimacy. Penrose's calm juxtapositions of antinomies seem to take direct inspiration from Sappho. Where Sappho writes:

> I would rather see her lovely step
> and the motion of light on her face
> than chariots of Lydians or ranks
> of footsoldiers in arms[3]

Penrose follows:

So the drawing-rooms crumbled with the brightest
blonde combatants
Dying on the empty street in the barbaric squares
The mirrors the stucco the hoar frost commingling.
Day. No spear has even yet ripped the silk
You were there I did love you.[4]

Born under Capricorn on the first day of the year 1898,[5] Penrose's early years, spent in the French countryside of Mont-de-Marsan and Condom-sur-Baïse, were governed by rigid military and religious structures from which she sought escape—her father, Colonel Maxime Boué, served as a captain in the 34th Infantry Regiment during the First World War, and her mother, Susanne, was a devout Catholic. Prior to the outbreak of war, Valentine attended high school at the prestigious Maison de la Légion d'Honneur in Saint-Denis.[6] Her ambitions, however, lay elsewhere. Her friend and collaborator, the poet Roy Edwards, posits that her first poem was in fact "an aborted flight to Paris in order to join the Folies Bergères" in a bid to leave her "loved but irritating" life with her parents.[7] Penrose embodied the stubborn ambition of the mythical sea goat, the creature that signals the tenth sign of the Zodiac. The hybrid sea-goat's top half represents Capricorn—the figure of the trepidatious goat as an earth sign, with its ruling planet, Saturn—while its bottom half, in surrealist terms, represents the deep, watery unconscious. Taken together, the ability to master both land and sea aptly describes Penrose, the shape-shifting poet voyager. The link to her past through her birth sign was evidently a preoccupation throughout her life, featuring in her poetry from *Herbe à la lune* (Moon Grass, 1935) to her final collection, *Les Magies* (Sorceries, 1972). The poem "Capricorn" is a direct reference to the night of her birth:

I am on a bench as the sparrowhawk perches
An old uniform fading in the branches.

And I think about captains
Whose wife supplicating and suffocating gives birth
In front of the window
By January night.

The narrator is distanced from the scene she imagines, yet tangible traces—the military frigidity in the air, a circling bird of prey that comes to rest, the haunting trace of a uniform—manifest in the present, as if the view from the bench is a front row seat to this fantasy. And, as in so many of Penrose's poems, a raw energy is accompanied by sensory impressions of temperature, the sky, and the odor of the animal kingdom, all comingling. Her poetry creates sentience and presence that bridges the human, animal, mineral, and botanical, both living and dead.

In 1916 Penrose's artistic curiosity took her to Paris, where she enrolled to study drawing at École des Beaux-Arts.[8] By the 1920s she had found her calling—writing poetry, which soon drew the attention of surrealist Paul Éluard. She attended lectures on art and culture at La Sorbonne and studied Sanskrit alongside what was then known as "oriental philosophy." In the words of her niece Marie-Gilberte Devise, "elle était très marquée par l'Inde" (She was deeply affected by India)[9]; the influence of India would last her entire life. When she later married the British surrealist artist and curator Roland Penrose, she wore an Indian sari (possibly loaned by neighbors in France who had visited India[10]), and archival photographs show her wearing this garment during her later visits to India. What for some might have been an affectation, or ill-advised cultural appropriation, was for Valentine a serious commitment to her values.

She traveled far and wide, never seeming to stay in one place for long. She crossed the Himalayas, journeying through the Indian subcontinent, Kenya, Egypt, Tenerife and the Canary Islands, and across parts of Southern, Central, and

Eastern Europe over several decades. She craved adventure, yes, but also new routes to spiritual wisdom and liberation. Her voyages from the mid-1930s onward refuse any stereotypical definition of the white European tourist. While unquestionably privileged and financially supported, Penrose truly sought to understand the cultures of the places she visited. She inhabited various roles over the following decades: an ashram disciple, a disguised pilgrim attempting to enter Tibet, a volunteer soldier, a student of philosophy, alchemy and astrology, a spiritual guide, and an adventurer. But to read Penrose's sorcery and uncanny powers of divination as being unserious, or distant from social reality, would be an error. She desperately felt that a call to action was necessary for artists and writers. Resolutely antifascist, humanitarian, and nonconformist, she volunteered for the Free French Forces and was stationed in Corsica and Algeria during the Second World War, having already served as a driver during the London Blitz (1940–41) after being rerouted on a return trip from India. She was also a cosignatory of the British Surrealist Group's "Declaration on Spain" (1936) in protest at the escalating Spanish Civil War. For this reader, the dark, nagging threat of violence within this context makes the spiritual, mythic, and esoteric elements of her language even more profound.

In "Madwoman of Sargassum," the opening refrain is repeated in the final stanza, wrapping the poem into a cautionary tale:

> Do not look back forlorn
> Toward the bitter orange tree.

The imperative condenses place, time, race, and grief, and ensures that the would-be voyager at the center of the poem, heralded by hopeful mountain birds, will forever be tempted and taunted by the past. Penrose sailed many times during her lifetime and, as her poems indicate, these voyages held a curious temporality in which the present moment, infused with time from the past and future, became a threshold space where she could think and collate disparate and wide-ranging philosophies. She writes of the cultural belief systems that she encountered while a disciple at the Sri Aurobindo ashram in Pondicherry,[11] for example; and on a layover in Mombasa, she dreams of the African city before Portuguese colonization.[12]

Fascinated by mythological as well as astronomical readings of the stars, Valentine Penrose's contribution to surrealism's engagement with the occult is significant. André Breton acknowledged that she brought "the basics of astrology" to his attention in 1927.[13] Penrose, with Pierre Mabille, Charles Fourier, and Emile-Jules Grillot de Givry,[14] "is mentioned in Breton's response to a survey posted by the International Centre for Astrology in 1954, and her detailed astrological birth chart for Max Ernst is among Breton's manuscripts."[15] Penrose also drew individual birth charts for Pablo Picasso, Comte de Lautréamont, and Guillaume Apollinaire. Her studies in astrology and mythology can be seen in her collage work from very early in her career. For example, while living in France in the 1920s, she made a paper-collaged screen detailing astrological and mythological points on her version of the night sky.[16] This personal object—one imagines it decorating a bedroom or dressing room—brings the cosmos into everyday life, and the skies become close at hand.

Penrose's deep knowledge and skills in intuitive readings are evident across all periods of her poetry, and feature prominently in *Les Magies*, where stanzas brim with a cosmological sensitivity that is enriched by folkloric incantations, Hindu wisdom, and flora and fauna from her worldwide travels. Sometimes, Penrose's expansive ideas may appear together in a single poem, or even a single line: "I wept stars" ("The Flocks"); such is the interwoven tapestry of her poetic philosophy. In "The Templars of Pierrefitte," for example, the poet seems to imagine Templar knights through their fading historical significance, slumbering, perhaps, in an archive (the largest textual archive on the French Templars is in the National Archives at Pierrefitte-sur-Seine, from where the titular location may derive), surrounded by paraphernalia (the Masonic cross, heraldic ivy, Agnus Dei—the Lamb of God). Penrose had an interest in the gnostic lore of the Templars, and here the poem seems to take them into account as if they were protagonists in an Eastern story or verse.

From Christian orthodoxy to various occult and mystical spiritual approaches, Penrose expanded what she saw, heard, and felt through wider syncretic interpretation. She once articulated, in a letter to her friend Valentine Bonamy, that the life of the soul is tied to a celestial "assembly of gods" displayed in the seasonal rotation of the solar system. Describing the autumn waning of the moon and Saturn awakening on the horizon, a memory of the Himalayas prompts her to reflect on her approach to mysticism:

> I always remember so wise, so clear minded galarza [*sic*]. It is by you that we met him, remember . . . Fortunately I have all the notes of his teaching, and his book too—I read the German philosopher F. Schelling, too. It is more or less the same kind of philosophy: "The Ages of the World"—"Philosophy of Mythology." I think that it is the best approach towards the truth that we can reach here, such a wide scope.[17]

Penrose refers here to Vincente Galarza, Viscount of Santa Clara—born Vicente Galarza y Pérez Castañeda—an archaeologist-turned-mystic, with whom Roland and Valentine studied consciousness and universalism during their visits to Cairo in 1927, and Kolkata in 1932. The reference to Galarza alongside the works of Friedrich Wilhelm Joseph von Schelling is illustrative of Valentine's openness. Schelling's *Naturphilosophie*, for example, amplifies the agency and autonomy of the natural world, a theme of Penrose's poems; Galarza's philosophical view of human consciousness striving to dissolve its duality to finally be at one with the universe—a view drawn from a multitude of Egyptian and Indian sources—is tempered by Penrose with a surrealist emphasis on the self as conduit of the marvelous.

While her research shows profound and sustained engagement with philosophy and history, the poems have a lightness and an energetic charge of spontaneity. Archival manuscripts of her poems in draft form show few annotations, evincing a clarity and immediacy of thought.[18] This supports the view of her dear friend and peer, Éluard, who notes the certainty of her word choices: "Valentine Penrose never hesitates to write a word in the place of another, the immediately accessible word instead of the rebellious word. From this comes a poetically clear language."[19] In surrealist terms, accessing illogical, unconscious, or hidden aspects of lived reality is an essential motivation for the poet. But for Penrose, who also wrote automatic texts (for example, a transcription of a dream entitled "Rêve" [1927],[20] and the prose work *Le nouveau Candide* [1936]), this was just one facet of the mode of divination. A "nomadic verbal alchemist,"[21] she plunged into the veins of darker literary predecessors, transmuting female love and erotics, lore, and contradictory belief systems into new poetic tools: "The pentacle is a curriculum."

This practice stretches beyond the "completely raw"[22] images of automatic writing. For example, a poem from *Herbe à la lune* lays bare the ridges of conscious thought, of a woman finding pleasure in the prismatic possibilities of her life:

> the happy exchanges in her blue and red heart
> a giantess to ancient pluralities and to those she dreams
> drawers of drawers, mirrors of mirrors.

Mirrors and drawers—exposing and folding in the figure of the self—here represent the poet's experience of growing up with hope, while also being aware that the oppositional forces of ice and fire, death and life will never be reconciled (although many of Penrose's poems do try to reconcile them). Her friends cite Arthur Rimbaud's poetry as a guiding force in her poetry, and there are frequent mentions of him across her oeuvre, including in her letters: "Rimbaud's most beautiful poems came out of the gray bleakness of his childhood."[23] It is incredible to me how Penrose can be so light, generous, and hopeful in her formal experiments with such heavy materials. She never shies away from the difficult, emotional, or brutal realities of her life, and the life of the twentieth-century world. Instead, she brings lightness *with* the darkness, refusing sentimentality by rooting love in otherworldly, mysterious, and often nocturnal or transitional space and time.

Mia X. Pérez's translation of Penrose's collected poems into English feels prescient, urgent, even, at a time when our world needs magical thinking. It is over a century since a 26-year-old Valentine entered her poem, "Pater," into a poetry competition (Le Jasmin d'argent) and won second place. Written in the interwar period, its critique of biblical themes through a poetic rewriting seems characteristic of her wider project of dismantling power and offering space to the female perspective. For the twenty-first-century reader, Penrose's knack for capturing the supernatural and ephemeral secrets of ordinary existence can provide alternative ways of experiencing and conceptualizing the world in an age of increasing economic, environmental, and political instability. I have been fortunate to study Penrose's life, and I have derived intense and galvanizing energy from it. I see her poetry as nonconformist, feminist, and rebellious. It is also challenging, requiring the reader to follow a series of capacious and intricate references. We should let them take us where they will, following their tensions and unravelings in much the same way that Penrose approached her voyaging: "This morning, even though I am so knowledgeable about flora and fauna, I was quite out of my depth, such strange plants, such disturbing creatures."[24] Her poems mirror the strange and disturbing; they cast spells, as this beautifully sensitive translation reveals, and these spells come at a time when interest in mystical and occult knowledge is growing in the Western world. Astrology, work with crystals and stone circles, Tarot reading, aura photography, and non-Western belief systems are being taken up by new practitioners as counterrevolutions in the everyday.

Valentine has long been recognized in surrealist history as the first wife of Roland Penrose, the friend of Picasso, Breton, Éluard, Eileen Agar, and many others. Her love affair with the painter and poet Alice Rahon has produced much speculation. To each of these friends, the skill of her poetry was always observed and underlined; they admired her greatly and often sought her advice on their own work. It is important that her influence as a poet and artist is more widely recognized, and this new volume of collected poems will reach readers who might be encountering her breathtaking poetry for the first time. Penrose's stanzas index a world inhabited by the female poet, she who navigates by her own coordinates, refusing any single belief system, or heteronormative formulas for love. Pérez's translation ensures that Penrose's poetry will find its rightful place in more prominent discussions of women surrealists, their work, and their philosophical solutions to the complexities of the human condition:

> The cards the blades the familiars
> The floorboards are being shuffled.[25]

Notes

1 Tulasi Srinivas, "Wondering about Wonder: An Introduction," in *Wonder in South Asia: Histories, Aesthetics, Ethics*, ed. Tualasi Srinivas (New York: State University of New York Press, 2023), 3, 10.

2 Penrose frequently places the figure of the "madwoman" in her poems—perhaps as a proxy for her own mental states over the years, but also as a figure of literary lineage that appeared in her research. She translated Jean Rhys's *Wide Sargasso Sea* (1966) into French, and dedicated a poem to Rhys, entitled "La Folle des Sargasses" ("Madwoman from over the Sargasso," 1968, published in *La Quinzaine Littéraire* and *Les Magies*, both in 1972. This translated title is Roy Edwards's; it is translated here as: "Madwoman of Sargassum"). Rhys reimagined Charlotte Brontë's Bertha Mason—the "madwoman in the attic" from Brontë's novel *Jane Eyre* (1847)—emphasizing her Creole ancestry, which Penrose also underscores in her poem. See Felicity Gee, "Framing the Voyage: Valentine Penrose, India, and the Geo-poetical," in *Valentine Penrose: Poet, Surrealist, Artist, Voyager*, ed. Felicity Gee, (London: Bloomsbury, 2026).

3 Sappho, *If Not, Winter: Fragments of Sappho*, trans. Anne Carson (London: Virago, 2002), 29.

4 Valentine Penrose, *Dons des féminines, Poems and Narrations*, ed. and trans. Roy Edwards (Manchester: Elephant Trust and Carcanet Ltd., 1977), 91.

5 Born Andrée Boué, on the draft certificate of her French marriage licence to Roland Penrose, Valentine is named as 'Madmoiselle Marcelle Marthe Marie Valentine Boué'. National Galleries of Scotland Archive, RPA GMA A35/1/1/RPA 455/1.

6 'Les maisons d'éducation' were schools for female pupils whose relatives had obtained the French Legion of Honor. The school at Saint-Denis was established by Napolean in 1803.

7 Roy Edwards, foreword to *Poems and Narrations* by Valentine Penrose, ed. and trans. Roy Edwards (Manchester: Elephant Trust and Carcanet Ltd., 1977), 2.

8 According to the obituary written upon Valentine's death by her brother Gilbert Boué. Thanks to Antony Penrose for providing me with this information.

9 'She was deeply affected by India', Marie-Gilberte Devise. interview with Antony Penrose, November 19, 1999. Marie-Gilberte, is the daughter of her brother Gilbert Boué.

10 As told to Antony Penrose, 'Interview with Giselle Aimon', Paris, 19 November 1999. Aimon is Valentine's cousin on her mother's side.

11 Aurobindo Ghose, (1872–1950), was a philosopher, poet, and Indian nationalist, and Mirra Alfassa, otherwise known as 'The Mother', were influential to Penrose's thinking. Penrose stayed at their ashram in Pondicherry on several occasions, but her visit between November 1935 and February

1936 was especially impactful. She writes fondly of her time spent there, and key concepts such as "Ananda" (bliss), "Nirvana," and "Agni" (fire) as well as Vedic gods, expansion of consciousness, and spiritual botany, enter her poetry over time.

12 Several of the letters in the Roland Penrose archive at the National Galleries of Scotland, Edinburgh were written onboard a cruise liner from India, or Africa, and offer us insight into her writing practice and thought processes while moving through water.

13 For unknown reasons, the line referencing Penrose's influence is stricken through on Breton's draft response to the survey, leaving only the impression that he began to build his knowledge of astrology in 1927 (citing thereafter a host of male artists and writers as inspiration). See André Breton, "Réponse à l'enquête du Centre international d'astrologie," André Breton Archives, https://www.andrebreton.fr/en/work/56600100384700 manuscript 577000. Accessed 21/02/2022. Breton worked on *L'Art magique* from 1953 until its publication in 1957, and this erasure of Penrose from his notes (literally striking out her name), despite having clearly recalled her centrality to these interests in astrology, seems to banish the feminine propensity toward occult and magical practices (see Ithell Colquhoun, Leonora Carrington, Alice Rahon, Remedios Varo, for example) to claim a different trajectory for his interests. As well as researching and drawing charts for Picasso and Ernst, Penrose constructed a retrospective birth chart for Guillaume Apollinaire, designed for the fiftieth anniversary of his death at the Institute of Contemporary Arts, London. See, *Guillaume Apollinaire 1880–1918: A Celebration 1968* (London: The Institute of Contemporary Arts, 1968).

14 The records, and some physical copies, of Roland and Valentine's book collection contain many books on esotericism, alchemy, witchcraft, and the occult, many in French. An annotated copy of *Raphael's Astronomical Ephemeris of the Planets' Places* was found in her desk drawer upon her death at Farleys Farm in Sussex, where she had lived on and off with Roland Penrose and Lee Miller since the 1950s. National Galleries of Scotland Archive, RPA A35/2/RPL1.

15 See Felicity Gee, "'The World Itself Stretches': Valentine Penrose, Beginnings, and Moons at Midday," *Valentine Penrose: Poet, Surrealist, Artist, Voyager* (London: Bloomsbury, 2026).

16 For more information on Penrose's astrological screen, see Felicity Gee, "'The World Itself Stretches': Valentine Penrose, Beginnings, and Moons at Midday," *Valentine Penrose: Poet, Surrealist, Artist, Voyager* (London: Bloomsbury, 2026).

17 Letter from Valentine Penrose to Valentine Dobrée, October 19, 1965, sent from Farley Farm, Sussex. Special Collections, Herbert Read Library, Brotherton Collection, University of Leeds. B.C. Dobrée correspondence, Item 11944.

18 Valentine's correspondence, drafts, notebooks, translations, tarot cards, ephemera, and personal effects at the time of her death, in 1978, are housed in the Roland Penrose Archive at the National Galleries of Scotland, Modern Art Two, Edinburgh.

19 Paul Éluard, preface to *Herbe à la lune* (Paris, G.L.M, 1935), trans. Mia X. Pérez.

20 "Rêve," *Cahiers du Sud* 91 (June 1927): 429–31. Two further automatic texts spilling from Penrose's dreams can be found among her papers in the archive and are reprinted in *Le Pin sur la lune et autres poèmes inédits*, ed. Séverine Orban (Liège: Presses Universitaires de Liège, 2022), 99–105.

21 As described by Penelope Rosemont, ed., *Surrealist Women: An International Anthology* (London: The Athlone Press, 1998), 48.

22 André Breton, Paul Éluard, and Philippe Soupault, *The Automatic Message; The Magnetic Fields; The Immaculate Conception*, trans. David Gascoyne, Antony Melville, and Jon Graham (London: Atlas Press, 1997), 28.

23 Letter from Valentine Penrose to Roland Penrose, September 30, 1935, sent from Aiguillon. National Galleries of Scotland Archive, A35/1/1/RPA712/3/34.

24 Letter from Valentine Penrose to Alice Rahon, trans. Jane Lee, June 8, 1940, written aboard the *Viceroy of India* cruise liner on her way back to France, Alice Rahon Papers, 1859–2004, undated, The Getty Research Institute, Los Angeles, Accession no. 2021.M.10. The voyage on which this letter was written was famously rerouted to London, where she met Lee Miller for the first time. See Roland Penrose, *Scrap Book 1900–1981* (London: Thames & Hudson, 1981), 134–5.

25 Roy Edwards, "For Valentine Reading the Tarot." See Felicity Gee, "For Valentine Reading the Tarot: Valentine Penrose," in *Surrealism and the Tarot: A Love Story*, ed. Tessel Bauduin (Lopen: Fulgur Press, 2025), 144–9.

Of Thorn and Wing

Imagerie d'Épinal
(1926)

The Imagerie d'Épinal

I — Jacques Cartier

Mer Atlantique.

Profils sur voiles, toiles boréales :
« Grande Hermine », « Petite Hermine », « Émerillon »,
tiroirs gonflés sur les rayons d'équateurs ronds.

Les feuilles et les écorces grandissent,
massifs à l'ombre des îles de médecine.

François, le doux compagnon
tient sa main sur l'air, les pignons
et la transparence des pigeons de Chinon.

Les caravelles amazones,
et les vierges, dans l'eau qui dansent
sous les palmes, épaisses barques.

                                        Vers la France
se fournit un coin de garenne à peupliers.

Trois juillet, quinze cent trente-six, aux balcons croisés
de St-Malo (les épices aux ports du Nord),
les archers ouvraient la bouche ;
                                  à droite et à gauche,
dix chefs indiens tournaient la tête.

I — Jacques Cartier

The Atlantic.

Profiles upon sails, boreal canvases
Grand Hermine, Petite Hermine, Émerillon,
drawers swollen beyond the radiuses of round equators.

The leaves and bark grow,
indiscriminate in the shadow of medicinal islets.

François, sweet companion
holds his hand upon the air, the pinnacles
and the transparency of pigeons from Chinon.

Amazonian caravels,
and the virgins, in the water dancing
under the palms, brawny boats.

                                        Toward France
it reserves a corner of the warren for poplars.

July 3rd, 1536, on the filigreed balconies
of St. Malo (spices in the northern ports)
archers open the muzzle;
                                  right and left
ten indian chiefs turned their heads.

II —Émigrants

Les fiancés sur le port, aussi enrubannés
que les langues de devises, les oriflammes
de la frégate.

L'oiseau de paradis, souple, part sous les palmes.

Pour l'embarquement, un homme-trouvère joue ;
à Rouen, dans les pupitres du collège,
les mappemondes, et les cartes d'ancien monde.

Les fiancés se sont dit
des mots comme des perles sous les eaux,
entraînés par le fleuve de fruits et d'oiseaux.

Au bord du fort, les singes sont accroupis,
et la fiancée à panache recharge
les pistolets.
                                        Sur les nappes,
bougent les plumes des pirogues.

Mille lieues : la grande Mademoiselle fronde à Paris.

II — Emigrants

The betrotheds on the port, beribboned
like the parlances of proverbs, the pennons
of the frigate.

Supple bird of paradise disappears under the palms.

For the departure, a trouvère plays;
in Rouen, in the desks of the school,
the ancient world is mapped and charted.

The betrotheds muttered to one another
words like pearls beneath the waters
dragged by a river of fruits and birds.

At the perimeter of the fort, monkeys crouched,
and the promised woman in plumes reloads
her pistols.
                                        Upon the expanses,
advance the feathers of canoes.

A thousand leagues away: the great Mademoiselle pelts Paris

III — La Pérouse

Le botaniste de l'Île de Pâques,
et le géographe d'avril
montent chercher les simples :

une australe étoile.

L'anneau de l'équipage, la plage
et les frégates sur les anses.
Quelques hommes doux commencent
des signes.

Adam pose son pied nu sur les veines d'arbres.

Ce matin, le long
des ponts, pour les parfumeurs de la Reine,
les carrosses,
la goutte d'eau des roseraies
courant les fils de Versailles ; les
mappemondes, les bougies encore allumées.

III — La Pérouse

Easter Island's Botanist
April's geographer
they rise in search of curatives:

                                        antarctic star.

The banner of the corps, the shore
the frigates in the bays.
Several gentlemen sound
their signals.

Adam sets his bare foot upon the tree veins.

That morning all along
the decks, for the perfumers of the Queen:
the carriages,
        the drop of rose water
rushing the bloodlines of Versailles; maps
of the world, candles still burning.

Herbe à la lune
(1935)

Moon Grass

VEINES NOUS DESCENDANT comme des mappemondes
donc nous vouerons à l'eau
tout le bleu de nos corps
s'il pleut.

Une grotte est ouverte
sur les monts Ararats
et la pluie devant elle
la pluie mâle et femelle
comme deux hirondelles.

Non parlante de dieu non parlante du feu
nous voici
contenant ton juste titre
eau de tout enchantement
eau qui bleuit à la mort
dame du sang.

VEINS CARVE THROUGH us like maps of the world
        so we will vow to the water
        all the blue of our bodies
                                        if it rains.

A gaping grotto
in the Ararat mountains
before it the rain
the rain male and female
like two swallowtails.

Not speaking of god not speaking of fire
we are here
holding your rightful title
water of every delight
water which turns blue upon death
        lady of blood.

Descendant aux abîmes
par des échelles des pluies dorées des rutiles et des aiguilles
les verticales du sommeil
les plus grandes plantées dans toutes les langues du monde
les autres dans toutes les graines du monde
avec leurs horticultures en dedans

mes propres lames dans chacun de mes débris
                                        j'arrive
      pollen du pôle noir.

Descending into the abyss
by ladders of gilded rains by rutile and by needles
the verticals of sleep
the largest rooted in all the world's tongues
the others in all the world's seeds
with their internal horticultures

my own blades, in every single one of my remnants
                                                          I arrive
        pollen from the black pole.

Belle galène hélène des maisons de Saturne
plombagines sauvagines
toutes sourdes orphelines
à l'Oural gîte éluvial.

Le pentacle est un programme
dont tous les bords se défont
lacs d'amour lacs de bétail et lacs d'aurone

femelle mangez trois feuilles
trois pierres font six maisons.

C'est ainsi que naissent feuilles
et au troupeau les ânesses
au géode les portées
dont tous les bords se défont

C'est alors que naissent hommes.

Elegant galena the Helen of Saturn's houses
black lead wildfowl
all deaf orphans
in the Urals dwell eluvial.

The pentacle is a curriculum
whose every edge disintegrates
lakes of love of livestock of southern wormwood

                female you eat three leaves
                three stones make six houses.

This is how the leaves are born
and in the herd the jennets
in the geode the litters
whose every edge disintegrates

While here arise men.

HOMME
en rêve plusieurs fois par moi assassiné
entre tes femmes main droite main gauche
pourtant libres jusqu'aux points cardinaux comme
[des blanches

et la plus belle que tu cèles
l'autre cher levant dame des grands vents fleur que
[j'aime tant
elle aussi bleu ciel dieu !

MAN
murdered by me several times in dreams
between your women, right and left
but free until the cardinal points like whites

and the most beautiful whom you conceal
the other lady of the great winds, flower that I love so
                    she as well sky-blue god!

À LA LÉGÈRE de leurs grands anges de liberté matés
aimer brûlot affamé
entre l'aimant et l'aimé.

Les prénoms sur l'eau de voyance
se portant et se rapportant leurs cœurs mineurs
à la santé du bonheur du jour du tien du mien.

Tranchant des rasoirs éclat des miroirs beauté de l'ivoire
tiroirs d'amour et d'oubli
la belle dormant tenant
la porte
les échanges contents dans son cœur bleu et rouge
géante aux vieux pluriels et à ceux qu'elle rêve
les tiroirs des tiroirs les miroirs des miroirs.

Donnez-moi l'épée de paradis.

Heedless of their somber angels of freedom
love aching incendiary
between the lover and the loved.

Names on the scrying water
bearing and comparing their minor hearts
to the health of the stars of the day of yours of mine.

Razors' edge mirrors' silver ivory's charm
drawers of love and oblivion
sleeping beauty holding
the door
the happy exchanges in her blue and red heart
a giantess to ancient pluralities and to those she dreams
drawers of drawers, mirrors of mirrors.

Give me the sword of paradise.

Langues de feu à la prairie
encor trop mortes du cela et du ceci
laissez danser.

Le bonjour et le bonsoir
l'ouvre toi le ferme toi
se débattaient au ciel noir.

La reine au moins a deux bras
pour se défendre du roi.

Couronne prix de raison
rien à voir avec ce sésame
héritage d'un seul ange.

Le cercle fermé le rocher fermé
veines terminées et sang prisonnier de poids condamné
race de ma roue

je suis vivant je suis vivante.

TONGUES OF FIRE in the prairie
alas too dead from that and from this
let us dance.

The good day and the goodnight
the open yourself the close yourself
battle in the dark sky.

At least the queen has two arms
to defend against the king.

Crown prize of reason
nothing to do with that open sesame
legacy of a single angel.

The closed circle the closed rock
drained veins and blood prisoner of weight locked away
breed of my breaking wheel

I am alive, I am a life.

Grenier de la belle émue
caverne des ours mâchant
terriers de race brune
gîtes de l'eau dispersée
gîtes de tous les étés
dans vos maisons lunaisons
adieu filles d'honneur.

Facettes des odeurs et midi et minuit
orient occident facettes de mes yeux
oui et non adam ève
bientôt je me tiendrai entre feu et une eau
avec la santé totale de l'or.

Attic of flustered beauty
cavern of gnawing bears
burrows of brown species
lairs of dispersed water
lairs of all the summers
lunations in your mansions
farewell maids of honor.

Facets of odors and midday and midnight
east and west facets of my eyes
yes and no adam eve
soon I will stand between fire and one water
with the wholesome vigor of gold.

LE DATURA LE serpent
la vie de mon sang
équateur de ce parc de seulement vingt ans.

À votre écorce d'ange
mes sept filles de l'ogre
je suis belle cathédrale
sur les tapis de moi-même.

À l'encre du feu de mes yeux
en cercle
sont écrits mes jeux
ceux-là même d'Adam

en cercle
touchera le serpent touchera le rocher
    la fille de la terre
    au ciel son capricorne.

THE DATURA THE serpent
life of my blood
equator of this park of only 20 years.

In your angel's bark
my seven daughters by the ogre
I am a beautiful cathedral
on the carpet of myself.

By the fire ink of my eyes
in a circle
my games are written
unchanged since those of Adam

in a circle
to touch the serpent to touch the rock
        daughter of the earth
        to heaven her capricorn.

Il paraît en forme de roi
chaque couleur plus égoïste qu'une autre
tous les oiseaux du monde au jardin de mon père
tous les oiseaux qui ont leur nid au monde.

Le rocher gluant le lierre le gui
sept femmes pendues au cachot du lierre
l'araignée en suspens au sagittaire
        qui crie de nuit :

en forme de roi ma vie en moi je ne te retiens pas.

IT TAKES THE form of a king
each color more solipsistic than the next
all the world's birds in the garden of my father
all the birds that nest in the world.

Slimy stone the ivy the mistletoe
seven dangling women hung in the ivy dungeon
the spider dangles in sagittarius
        which cries by night:

in the form of a king my life within me you I do not apprehend.

À LA NOURRICE qui conduit
pour moi l'histoire du trèfle
pour d'autres leurs préférences
tant qu'elles tiennent dans la nuit ou dans le jour.

Mère au bord des roseaux tendre apocalyptique
tes seins plaints par tes yeux de feuilles et de tigre
                    ma terre te dit non
                    mes quatre conflits te disent non
et mes parentes parts d'étoiles tombent du ciel
                    reprenant ma naissance.

For the nurse who performed
for me the tale of clover
for the others their preferences
so long as they last through night or day:

Mother at the edge of reeds tender apocalyptic
your breasts bereft in your leaf and tiger eyes
                my earth tells you no
                my four wars tell you no
and my kindred fragments of stars fall from the sky
                reclaiming my birth.

La pluie retrouvant ce qui est perdu
le soleil trouvant ce qui luit
grandes compagnes de ma vie.
Sur la terre qui est brune
moi aussi j'ai trouvé place.

    Aux sphères entières
    mouvant les tourments
par mes pas dorés je monte et descends.

Et s'y tiennent debout les eaux comme des lames
et plongerai ma lame au profond des citernes
sous mes yeux faux témoins au pays de mon être
dans la salle dormant à ma propre lumière
parmi tous les miroirs dont je me souviendrai.

THE RAIN RECOVERING what was lost
the sun finding what shines
great companions of my life.
On this brown earth
I too have found space.

        To the perfect spheres
        pushing torments
with golden steps I rise and fall.

And there the waters remain upright like blades
and I will drive my blade deep into the cisterns
under my eyes false witnesses to the countries of my being
in the room asleep within my own light
among every mirror I will remember.

Triste je suis là
accablée de fruits
de monnaies sans cours
et de tant de feuilles comme une terre

accablée de l'air
accablée de chair
et d'un feu couvant détestable ami.

Les poivres d'amour ont jeté l'oubli
leur cendre est tombée
le sang de mon sort m'a jeté la vie
ma vie est venue.

Triste je suis là
sur elle
l'accablée d'écorces et de fleurs aussi
du sort de ses règnes
du sort des étoiles.

Sad I am there
burdened with fruits
untendered currencies
as many leaves as an earth

burdened breath
burdened by flesh
and by a fire smoldering odious friend.

The spices of love have showered oblivion
their ash has fallen
the blood of my fate has cast life upon me
my life has come.

Sad I am there
atop her
she is heavy with barks and flowers too
with the fate of her dominion
the fate of stars.

Ainsi l'or et l'eau sentant bon sous la terre
vous comblent plantes du baume tranquille
l'opium des armoiries
et les satins brochés
et les souliers lilas
aux sucres des jardins
ont rattaché les miens.

« Dessous un rosier blanc il y a une princesse
blanche comme la neige belle comme le jour ».

Toi substance du jour
et substance du cœur
sucre et rosier
pareils comme des lièvres

allez allez maudits au cher mois de Marie.
Esprit du troupeau souviens-t'en et de la terre souviens-t'en
face jour blanc.

So, GOLD AND water odorous beneath the earth
plants lavish you with calming salve
opium of family crests
brocaded satins
lilac slippers
mine laced with
garden sugars.

"Beneath a white rose is a princess
white as snow and beautiful as day."

You substance of the day
substance of the heart
sugar and rose
the same as hares'

go! my wretched ones to the precious month of Mary.
Spirit of the flock and of the earth remember that
face day white.

Qu'y avait-il sur terre
qu'as-tu laissé dans le sillage
c'est le sillon que j'ai laissé
autour du vieux château tracé
au château la rose d'or était debout contre le mur.

Qu'y avait-il sur terre
peut-être des êtres
dans le sillon dans le sillage
qu'eux-mêmes faisaient pour eux-mêmes.

Mais sûrement ce qu'il y avait
de l'herbe rase et puis haute
des chants dedans
des chansons tues et d'autres nées
des colliers de chants pour l'année

O cercle cette herbe ces chants cette rose.

What was there on this earth
what have you left in the wake
it's the tread I left
around the old castle leading
to the castle the golden rose lined up against the wall.

What was there on this earth
could be some beings
in the tread in the trail
that they themselves made for themselves.

But certainly there was
low grass then high
singing within
silenced melodies and others born
necklaces of song per yearly cycle

O circle this grass these songs this rose.

Il est le feu il brûle et je suis l'eau je noie
ô froide fille.
La terre est mon amie
la lune aussi sa servante
ainsi nous visitant au fond de nos cavernes
nos repos nos langueurs loin de tout accoudées
nous passons longuement les nuits à nous connaître
autour de nos trois feux mystérieux et frères.

J'ai les plus belles fleurs
j'ai le plus beau mirage
j'ai le plus beau miroir
je suis l'eau qui se chante.

He is the fire he burns and I am the water I drown
o cold daughter.
The earth is my intimate
the moon her servant
visiting us like so at the floor of our caves
our rest our languor far from everything
we spend much of the night getting to know one another
around our three mysterious fires and brothers.

I possess the most beautiful flowers
I contain the most beautiful mirage
I hold the most beautiful mirror
I am the water who sings.

RONDES PLUMES ROND soleil
la boule du feu de joie
je m'étrangle de ma joie.
Douce femme douce au lac
l'air si tendre à ce satin.

Au milieu de moi tu bats
ô toi qui me noues au jour.

ROUND FEATHERS ROUND sun
bullet from rounds of joy
I choke on my joy.
Soft woman soft at the lake
the air so tender against the satin.

You pulse through me
o you who binds me to the day.

DANS LES TRIOMPHES passagers
des sèves et des sucs légers
au sommet de tours orangées
quand les lumières sont semées

tirez-moi mes anges
par vos fils oranges.

In the short-lived victors
of saps and subtle liqueurs
high atop oranged towers
when the lights are scattered

    pull me out my angels
    by your orange threads.

Goa I

Terre à tout faire terre à faire les pierres
verte et rouge qui gît terre à faire les graines
entre tes dents rongées geignent des cathédrales
au fond des sols moisis où les bananiers gîtent
l'Indienne tord sa robe à ce puits catholique.

Le Portugal s'accoude aux volutes de plâtre
sous l'huile de coco tendant ses doigts ridés
à l'eau bénite au fond des cloîtres délavés
par les moussons roulant sur les autels dorés.

Terre à tous les miroirs
à toutes les fenêtres
tu tiens le Portugal dans ta dent rouge et verte
et la nacre et le rat.

Tes aisselles de palmes
ont des senteurs que jette en arrière le vide
que font et que défont tes seins noirs d'Indienne.
En ta robe dorée et tenant tous tes cierges
l'huile du Portugal des morts des repentirs
les bijoux effondrés aux sacristies des jungles
tandis que tu reposes
dans tes chambres du Sud tendues de mousselines
les pestes et les plâtres aux mantilles en miettes
font ici leur accord.

Que vois-tu je vois mes filles
que vois-tu je vois des mères
je vois mes filles les tiges
mordant leurs fibres amères
je vois mes filles les pierres

Goa I

Earth that births all earth that births stones
green and red here lies the earth that births grain
between your ground teeth are lamenting cathedrals
on the bottom of moldy floors where banana trees lie
the Indian wrings her dress in this Catholic well.

Portugal leans upon plaster plumes
underneath coconut oil extending its fingers wrinkled
from holy water at the bottom of cloisters faded
from the monsoons rolling over golden altars.

Earth to all mirrors
to all windows
you hold Portugal in your green and red tooth
and the mother-of-pearl and the rat.

                                        Your palmy armpits
contain fragrances thrown back by the void
made and unmade by your dark Indian breasts.
In your golden dress holding your altar candles
Portugal's oil of death and repentance
broken jewels in the sacristies of jungles
all the while you rest
in your southern rooms draped with muslin
the plagues and the plasters with shredded shawls
        here reach an accord.

        What do you see I see my daughters
        what do you see I see mothers
        I see my daughters the stem
        biting their bitter fibers
        I see my daughters the stones

sur l'église catholique
et les cramoisis tes frères
pendus aux granges des pierres.

Et moi la grande parente
ici laissée sans mantille
les salpêtres et les argents
moines desservants ici
moi terre de partout c'est ainsi que je vis.

on the catholic church
and the crimsons your friars
hung from the stone granges.

And myself the great parent
here left without a shawl
the saltpeter and the silvers
monks and vicars here
myself the land of everywhere this is how I live.

Goa II

Sur le fleuve de lait aux cieux doux traversés
s'élèvent des plis et des cassures de linges
des mains jointes des yeux bouillonnent sur les berges
les saintes en pleurs courent dans le vent léger.

Mais les façades sont allées aux Canaries
du scorpion du serpent monte la fine odeur
quand moisit la banane au pied du mur au nord
le linge de la sainte à Goa se pourrit.

Les céramiques ont goûté
ton ivoire tourmenté
dans les cloîtres épicés
ton héroïque beauté
seule d'os dans les plâtres émiettés.

Je parlerai du vent ô toit des feuilles sur le monde
je parlerai des nuits je parlerai des cèdres
des vestiges avant de naître
de ces enfants pressés aux strates des montagnes
nains tortueux et présents dont nous sommes les fils
atteints partout au cœur.

Vaincus à reculons repassant nos obstacles
nous voici revenus au cirque savoureux
où l'huile de l'ancêtre et du beau ténébreux
oint silencieusement la face des basaltes.

Je te vole à nouveau puits endormi des mères
cirque où les antérieurs s'écoulent et se nomment
où la géante aux seins noirs dans des laits nocturnes
gave de blonds néants afin qu'ils se souviennent.

Goa II

Upon the river of milk with sweet spanning skies
fractures and folds of linen arise
hands joined boiling eyes on the banks
weeping saints run through the breeze.

But the facades have gone to the Canaries
from the scorpion and serpent a fine odor emanates
when the banana molders against the wall to the north
the saint's cloth decays in Goa.

The ceramics have savored
your tortured ivory
in the spiced cloisters
your heroic beauty
only bones in the crumbled plaster.

I will speak of the wind o roof of leaves atop the earth
I will speak of nights I will speak of cedars
of prenatal vestiges
of these children rushed to the mountainous stratum
dwarves devilish and present of which we are the children
touched throughout the heart.

Defeated we withdraw passing our obstacles once more
here we have returned to the delectable circus
where the oil of ancestors and the dark and comely
silently anoint the basalt face.

I steal you anew sleeping wells of mothers
circus where the befores flow by and name one another
where the giantess with dark breasts in the nocturnal milks
fills blond oblivions so that they might remember.

Souvenu revenu me voici dans mes bras
puisant aux vieux filons doux comme les panthères
tournant au fond du cirque où le possible ciel
n'a pas encore plaqué son pesant sortilège.

Les nouvelles vapeurs des soufres
les nouvelles vapeurs d'étoiles
les blondes
tout ce qui se tient
                    ce qui se tiendra
berce-le bien ô grande berce-le bien !

Remembered returned here I am in my arms
summoning with the ancient maneuvers gentle like the panther
spinning at the bottom of the circus where the potential sky
has not yet laid its oppressive spell.

Fresh vapors of sulfur
fresh vapors of stars
blondes
all that remains
                    that will remain
nurture it well o great mother nurture it well!

Sainte Luce sainte Claire
vous rencontrant aux fontaines
piquée de plumes vertes
        dis-le-moi source.

        Mon cœur est souple
        aux osiers blancs
        je bats je tourne
        le blanc le vert.

Elle ondule celle aux bras blancs
loin de l'horrible pierre et mouillée dans les sables
la terre suffisant loin de toute salure
et l'eau de pluie la tourne en fuseau neuf de bulbe.

        Glisse et lisse le prêle
        le peuplier le saule
        ô mes filles montez
        l'air jaune de l'été.

        Une croix de paille au cœur
        au bas de toutes
        les cheveux distraits je règne
        nul ne me soulèvera
            verte verte.

SAINT LUCY SAINT Claire
meeting you at the fountains
pricked by green quills
        tell me the source.

        My heart is supple
        within the withies
        I beat I spin
        the white the green.

She flutters the one with white arms
beyond the horrible stone and dampened in the sands
abundant land far from any salinity
and the rainwater turns fresh spindles from the bulbs.

        Slip and slicken the horsetail
        the poplar the willow
        o my daughters climb
        summer's yellow air.

        Straw cross upon the heart
        at the bottom of all
        dreaming hair I reign
        with none to overthrow me
           green green.

Les pompes rousses et les plâtres
brûlant les gorges remontez
l'épaule sèche de l'été
grésille de palais qui ne sont pas hantés.

Où le vent tourne dans sa paume
les cloches tendres
les saluts verts
officinale la géante
et les reines les rois sont là.

Red pitcher pumps and plasters
Burning the throats try higher
the dry shoulder of summer
crackles from unhaunted palates.

Where wind cycles in its palm
the tender bells
the green salutes
apothecary giantess
and the queens and kings are all there.

AYANT ÉCARTÉ MA surface
tordant encore au bout de mes bras inconnus
des cheveux à venir de périmés visages
un lot phosphorescent de plages et de puits.

Ainsi je fleurirai debout selon ma fleur
géante aux yeux tournants étonnés sans coutumes
et une de se sentir dans les suds amoureux
retranchée des chaleurs poisseuses et des plumes.

Aux fenêtres du ciel volent les mousselines
et les pistils poudreux ont éclaté forgés.

Creuse autour d'elle la forêt les branches se coupent
creuse autour d'elle le désert les flammes s'interrogent
creuse autour d'elle la terre les pierres se relèvent.

> Couronne d'épine et d'ailes
> cercle de charbon de cendre
> tombez robes autour d'elle
> collines neige et comètcs
> lances et cendres par terre.

Elles les pieds sur le cœur sûrement
nourrie parcourue montante.

Having split apart my surface
still wringing at the end of my strange arms
hair to grow from outworn faces
a phosphorescent fate of shores and wells.

So I will bloom upright according to my flower
a giant with spinning eyes amazed unhabitual
and a sensation of being in the amorous souths
taking refuge from sticky heat and feathers.

In the windows of the sky muslins fly
and powdery pistils have erupted fully forged.

Rooting around her the forest the branches cross
Rooting around her the desert the flames ponder
Rooting around her the earth the stones elevate.

> Crown of thorn and wing
> circle of coal and ash
> fall you gowns around her
> hills snow and comets
> lances and ashes aground.

She her feet surely on the heart
nourished traveled ascended.

Armagnac

Et mieux que vous gardé les infinies douceurs
des sœurs au doigt de verre au ciel écoutant tout
l'inca versé à l'ouest parmi les anémones
comme un pagne battant le vent d'ouest au côté.

Une roue dans le sable a monté vers l'orage
et la sœur blanche en haut assise sous le chêne
patiemment les pains ronds attendent sous les chênes
quand remuent les fossiles au souvenir d'orage.

Il est l'œil de la terre étouffé sous les lianes
un étang accueillant comme une gorge beige
où grognent les géants oubliés à la traîne
de la dame portant ailleurs insouciante
par-dessous le soleil son cou tendu de reine.

        Si chaud le crapaud
        comme un pain de vase.
Pains de terre aiguilles de terre
se défaisant comme des mies dans cette flaque.

La liane est tombée verte et la lumière aussi
les yeux ont brillé vert et jaune et les mares
les deux grandes mains de la terre se sont jointes
et les deux mains de l'eau et des proches parentes.
Sur le sein d'herbe voyez-les ces jeunes filles
pures comme autrefois en robes rayées vertes.

        Bouillant et vert
        le crapaud vert
        de l'Armagnac

Armagnac

And more than you watched over the infinite sweetnesses
of the sisters their glass fingers in the sky
listening to all the Inca poured into the west among the
        anemones
like a slip beating the west wind alongside.

A wheel in the sand rose toward the storm
and the white sister sat above under the oaks
patiently the round loaves wait under the trees
as fossils stir at the memory of thunder.

The eye of the land smothered beneath the lianas
an inviting pool like a beige throat
where giants groan forgotten trailing behind
the woman carelessly carrying elsewhere
from below the sun her neck strained with regality.

        Toad so hot
        like a cake of mud.
Dirt cakes dirt needles
dissolving in that puddle like crumbs.

The liana fell green and so too the light
the eyes shone green and yellow and the pools
the two great hands of the earth joined
and the two hands of water and close kin.
On the grass breast look at them these young daughters
pure as before in green streaked dresses.

        Boiling and green
        green toad
        of Armagnac

et sifflant d'oubli le sanglot de vase
gorgée chaude comme ma mère étais-tu là.

hissing with oblivion the sob of silt
submerged hot like my mother were you there.

UNE EAU DANS la forêt
une tache au pelage
une rose foncée un oiseau de couleur.

Voici à vous mes mains à tous les coins de l'air
je toucherai partout les cristaux enfantés
de la nuit du château à cette aube d'été.

Au sourd
de velours
dans l'arbre les bougies.
Celui qui rôde est-il
descendu dans les nappes
au bas des grands repas des blés et des rousseurs.

Mais loin des douceurs
piétinant le feu
la source d'airain
au milieu du feu
au milieu du pain
ne buvant la soif ne mangeant la faim
l'ange sans couture et qui n'a pas faim.

Body of water in the forest
stain on the hide
darkened rose, colorful bird.

For you my hands in all corners of the air like so
I will reach far and wide crystals born
From the chateau night to this summer dawn.

With velvet
deafness
candles in the tree.
The one who roams has he
gone down into the cloths
beneath the large meals the grains and freckles.

    But far from comforts
    stomping out the fire
    the bronze spring
    at the center of the fire
    at the center of the loaves
not drinking his thirst not eating his hunger
seamless angel who does not yearn.

Du Sinaï plein de cornes
qui consument et détonnent
je me détourne et vois ton paysage.

Des mères de la montagne
de ce sang plein de cratères
des feux du cœur
des plans des plumes des crêtes
des rayures de toisons
je me détourne et vois ton paysage.

La pluie du ciel a pris le large
le bras du corps a pris le large
dans l'été qui tourne et qui charge
les pollens de ses floraisons
et les poudres en rond se cabrent.

Tous les astres ont pris le large
voici la ligne et voici l'ange.

Laissez voler ces plumes
ces mois et ces parcelles
que les mille rayures
abandonnent la cime
et qu'un diamant repose
seul comme une eau sans cause
entre l'aube et le soir.

FROM MANY-HORNED SINAI
devouring and discordant
I turn away to gaze upon your scenery.

From mothers of the mountain
from this blood pocked with craters
from fires of the heart
from blueprints feathers peaks
from strips of fleece
I turn away to gaze upon your scenery.

Rain from the sky set sail
arms from their bodies set sail
in the summer that churns and details
the pollens of its inflorescences
and the powders recoil in a circle.

All the stars set sail
here the line and here the angel.

> Let these feathers fly
> these months and these plots
> that the thousand scrapes
> abandon the peak
> and a diamond rests
> singular like water without a cause
> between the dawn and the dusk.

Sans pas sans bras tu danses
sans pas sans bras tu te remues
de tes antennes de tes mues.

Avec ton corps plein de signes magiques
de flammes bleues à gauche léchant l'eau
les germes en bride
le soleil hérissé à droite des épaules
ouest sauvage et d'attentifs carbones
au ras des prêles noirs suivant ta course

à l'écorce tu écoutes
la sève t'écoute
la goutte t'écoute et pleut.

Aucun message interrompu
rien en suspens ni cœur battant
au cloître des arbres du vent
la procession cheminant et te connaissant.

Au ciel ils passent
flairent at continuent
dans l'eau savent en terre savent
si tu ris dans ce parc secouant ta crinière
à genoux le soleil le verseau et les salles
éblouissantes se suivant.

Sur les ailes qui portent
au cœur des poudres vertes
les doigts dans le silence
reposée tu t'enroules.

No steps no arms you dance
no steps no arms you sway
by your antennas your moltings.

With your body full of magic symbols
of blue flames to the left the water lapping
the bridled sprouts
the bristled sun the shoulders' right
wild west and watchful carbon
level with the black horsetail tracking your path

to the bark you listen
the sap listens back
the droplet listens and weeps.

Not one message interrupted
no bated breath nor beating heart
in the cloister of wind-blown trees
the procession moving and knowing you.

In the sky they pass
sniffing and continuing
in water they know in earth they know
whether you laughed in this park ruffling your mane
in succession the sun aquarius dazzling
galleries they kneel.

Carrying on the wings
green powders to the heart
fingers in the silence
rested you entwine.

DANS MES YEUX le feu de terre
rond et pris dans ses dentelles
au ciel de gauche m'entaillent
d'envahissantes médailles.

Et les cristaux au centre rouge ont pris la place
et des étoiles séparées qui se sourient
douces poussant devant elles le sang fleuri.

Là croît le pistil
au monde d'en face
les baguettes du plomb désert ont bourgeonné
les rejaillissements ont monté comme un blé
les yeux ont moissonné des lignes attelées
naissant persévérants de cœur vide pourtant.

Mon cœur me mange
ma bouche me mange
je reviens pourtant
me voilà brillante.

Enroulant déroulant éternelle ce lin
mes fils croisés mes astéries à tous les coins
les doigts renaissant de mes mains
au bal ardent des étamines dans le sein
tous couteaux de vie dans le cœur
de forêt perdue
ou de feu noyée.

Était-elle dans ces cercles se mordant
ou dans cette nappe totale tombant à dieu.

IN MY EYES the fire of earth
round and caught in its lace
in the sky from the left cutting me
with invasive decorations.

And the crystals in the red center took hold
and separated stars smile sweetly to one another
sprouting before them the flowered blood.

There grows the pistil
in the mirror world
the rods of desert lead budded
the surges again rose like wheat
the eyes have harvested harnessed lines
emerging tenacious from a heart however empty.

My heart eats me
my mouth eats me
still I return
here self-faceted.

Eternally folding unfolding this linen
my tangled threads my sea stars in every corner
fingers reborn from my hands
to the stamens' raging ball in the breast
all of life's knives in the heart
of lost forest
or drowned fire.

Was she in these circles biting herself
or in that total shroud falling toward god.

DE CE CŒUR inconscient à force de présages
de lumières debout
les feuilles en attente exigent ton miracle.

Les reines ont pétri la lueur engloutie
les clefs de danse en feu sont données au prairies.

        Ébranlé le levain
        et tourmenté le cercle
        sur la couleur à prendre
        hésite la clarté.
Près des yeux à venir insistent les lumières
les bêtes sont en rond autour la clairière.

S'ouvrira fleurira unique enfin de toi
tirant l'air et la bulle un globe montera
et vieille la tête d'airain resplendira
        par une nuit ô toi
signée d'incohérentes étoiles
en ordre et en désordre comme la forêt.

FROM THIS HEART careless after many omens
from standing lights
the waiting leaves demand your miracle.

The queens kneaded the submerged light
burning keys of dance were bestowed upon the meadows.

    The yeast rattled
    the circle tormented
    over the color to be taken
    clarity pauses.
Near the eyes to come the lights insist
the beasts in a circle round the clearing.

To finally open to bloom only from you
drawing the air the bubble a globe will arise
and the old bronze head will gleam
    that one night you were
marked with incoherent stars
in order and disorder like a forest.

Quand cette bête menue
se roule aux pieds des buveurs
quand arrivent les sabots
par le coup se ferme l'eau
quand rient aux meubles les rats avec les licornes
en plus petit ou plus grand que la main de Dieu

le château brûlant trop haut
l'aile à la flamme trop sournoise
l'eau trop pleine trop loin sournoise.

Loin des sangs encadrés et des saisons de flammes
étouffées de cotons de poils

la neige au bord du sang et le blanc pour le noir
étends tes bras à leur longueur
comme tu fus créée
rassemble l'air à sa douceur comme il est né
et pure au milieu de la salle

de lueur de fleur
au centre bat ta lueur
et de tes doigts quittant les peurs tu montes.

When this slender beast
rolls about the feet of drunks
when the hooves arrive
blow by blow the water retreats
when at the furniture rats and unicorns laugh
smaller or larger than God's hand
        the chateau burning too tall
        the burning wing too insidious
        the water too full too far insidious.

Far from framed blood and seasons of flames
snuffed out with bristles and cotton

the snow on the edge of blood as white is to black
extend your arms to their lengths
as you were created
conjoin the air to its sweetness as it was born
and pure at the heart of the room

        flower glowing glimmer
        your light pulsing in the center
you ascend and terrors fall from your fingers.

Je me fleuris en cercle comme une tiare comme une aube
ma main donne une étoile et une étoile l'autre
je parle aux étincelles.

À l'autel des forêts le sang éblouissant
au coin le lierre et puis le vent.

Monte rose la rose
de la terre où je penche avec des feuillages
au point d'un éclair vieux
monte et descend la hache.

        L'absence fleurira
        la hache montera
bientôt à l'horizon du fleuve voici l'eau neuve.

I FLOWER IN a circle like a tiara like a dawn
my hand unfolds one star and from that star another
I speak with the glimmers.

Dazzling blood on the altar of forests
in the corners ivy and then wind.

Ascending blush the rose
of the earth where I bend with the foliage
in the speck of an old light
the axe rises and falls.

        The absence will blossom
        the axe will be raised
on the horizon of the river new water soon will come.

Et je tombe à travers des lits
épuisée de chanter défaite
et des draps jaunes et des plis
m'accueillent suaires d'auberge.

Le mendiant là-haut troue au feu son manteau
au ciel miraculeuse et noire frappe une eau
aux granits empilés dort un bâton debout
titubant de bergers de portes et de loups.

La tête sur la plus haute lucarne
veillant là les peines de nuit
serrées comme des plis denses comme les pluies

donne prends voilà
le signe à ta porte
moi l'étoile je
passe des sacs noirs.

Il y eut des heures de tourelles et de disques et de croissants
en quel cirque perdu la légère poussière se souriant
sautant à l'eau sautant à terre à quelle porte éblouissants
naissant de matinée entière et ces disques et ces croissants.
Poussière au ciel légère quand
porte au cœur de signes couverte
grange de charmes neufs ouverte ?

AND I FALL across beds
exhausted from bellowing defeat
with yellow drapes and pleats
motel shrouds welcome me.

The beggar up there makes holes his coat in the fire
dark miraculous water strikes the sky
in granite heaps sleeps a standing staff
stumbling shepherds, ports, and wolves.

The head atop the highest dormer
there night's struggles keep vigil
packed like pleats dense like rain

give take like so
the symbol on your door
me the star I
pass from black bags.

There were hours of turrets and discs and crescent moons
in whose hopeless circus the fine dust smiling
leaping into the water into the earth into what door dazzling
emerging from morning whole and these discs and these moons.
Dust floating in the sky when
door at the heart sealed with symbols
grange by new charms opened?

Et cependant dessinant l'arabesque
des bras des fleurs
femme bruissante de feuillages
un seul luxe resté s'achevait dans les branches
un seul luxe sonnait sa fin de monde.

Ici ce point
entre deux doigts
ici la main
puisant le grain.

Au-dessus du grand blé les vrilles bleues atteignent
de lourds et frais oiseaux les ivraies étincellent
les feuilles aux grands revers blancs fières et belles
ne cèderont jamais le cœur des forteresses.

Et cependant le doux le vent
et cependant la douce l'eau
graines fondant graines coulant
le gris le tendre le verseau.

And yet tracing the arabesque
of arms of flowers
woman of susurrating foliage
one lone luxury remained fading in the branches
one lone luxury sounded her world's end

Here this point
between two fingers
here the hand
that gathers the grain.

Over the great grain blue tendrils reach
the birds heavy and cool the ryegrass sparkles
the leaves and their great white underbellies, proud and beautiful
will never cede the fortresses' heart.

And yet the gentleness the wind
and yet the sweetness the water
grains dissolving grains flowing
the gray the tender aquarius.

À LA VOIX des vivants qui sommeille réveille
et qui veille coupé de lames et de feuilles
de rayons transpercé
et qui veille enchanté le cercle l'endort.

Sous les traquenards aux plus basses branches
dans le premier langage noir criez au bord

si trouvant les sources
si bouche murée
si tête tragique
creux de toutes branches

crie la terre
crie son pain
crie sa pierre
heureuses pour l'eau chantent les baguettes blanches.

At the voices of the living the sleeping awaken
and wakeful cut by blades and leaves
by sunbeams pierced
and wakeful bewitched the circle lulls to sleep:

Beneath the ambushes among the lowest branches
in the first black language, cry at the edge

if finding springs
if muzzled mouth
if tragic head
hollow between all branches

cry the earth
cry her bread
cry her stone
white wands sing happily for the water.

De fulminantes croix de berger envahie
montant et s'abattant comme au nid les ailes
        un seul seigneur les tient
        dans une seule main.

Souviens-toi des épis des actes
de l'épanoui souviens-toi
du grand cercle fleuri en présents étalages
des fleurs à ce jardin de neiges et de rouge.

De mon front arrachée la montagne est restée
de la fronde lancés ah combien de présages
pétrissant obstinés de leurs mains à venir
d'eux-mêmes qui s'aimaient les prochains apanages.
Les feuilles ont frappé l'aile blanche du vent
la veine et la nervure au soleil transparent.
        Hausse la main
        hausse la feuille.

La terre de contours de couleurs et de tours
de fils jetés des tours menés et ramenés
de bonds pris et tombés la terre à toutes gouttes
d'une ignorante bouche
d'adorable nuit
de langage noire
voici la terre à elle-même s'est promise.

Overrun by fulminate shepherd crosses
rising and falling like wings in a nest
        a single master holds them
        in a single hand.

Remember ears of deeds
pleasures fulfilled remember
the large flowery circle opened in current display
of this garden of snowfalls and blush.

Torn from my brow the mountain stood
shot from the sling ah how many predictions
obstinately forging with fingers to come
from they themselves who loved one another the next estate.
The leaves struck the white wing of the wind
the vein and the rib transparent with sun.
        Raise the hand
        raise the leaf.

The land of contours colors and towers
children thrown from towers led away and then back
leaps taken and fallen the land in every droplet
from an ignorant mouth
of lovely night
of black language
here the land is promised to herself.

À mes carreaux nul n'a dansé
l'équateur a laissé la neige
sans venues l'appel des brasiers.

Au balcon sans fleurir les bouteilles de cendres
de grive d'or sont perdus les pouvoirs
dessein de terre terne guise
cette fois est toutes les fois
les épées sont remises
et si hantées les plantes au coin d'air ont douté.

Mais heureuse la dame peut toute au ciel bouger
et les nuits linges filants aux ronces courant
fleurs de cendre de ce côté sûr bien attisées
le lierre le vent le lierre le vent.

Upon my panes no one has danced
the equator has left the snow
without the comings the call of infernos.

On the balcony bloomless bottles of ashes
golden thrush their powers lost
earth's design drained charade
this time is every time
the swords are sheathed
and so haunted the plants wavered in the corner of air.

But happy the lady can move entirely in the sky
and the nights linens fraying in the coursing bramble
ashen flowers of this coast so thoroughly awoken
the ivy the wind the ivy the wind.

Ce n'est pas en vain les jambes dans la roue
les flammes les souffles changeant de voyelles
pas en vain triste par le grand soleil
perdue nue de soi pas en vain.

Tant de cercles de fleurs
bigarrées pour secret
et ce fil qui flottait
emporté par dieu sait.

Si ce parc d'aiguilles noires le nord la main sur son cœur
alors ces bordures blanches la joie sans la gagner.

À ce monde ce puits au mur les yeux tout grands
pour le peu de prise
l'eau entre les doigts
en vain qui le soleil ou l'ombre.

Une main sans revers
une main toute blanche
une main sans tenir.

It is not in vain the thighs in the wheel
the flames the breaths exchanging vowels
not in vain sad by the wide sun
lost shed from oneself not in vain.

So many circles of flowers
marbled for secret
and this drifting thread
carried away by God knows who.

If this black needle park the north the hand over its heart
then those white borders the unearned joy.

To this world this well to the wall eyes stretched wide
so to snatch a sliver
the water between the fingers
in vain: the sun or the shadow.

A hand without a palm
a hand completely empty
a hand without holding.

Tu remues tu brises
oiseau tu remues et brises

bernée de frondaisons
au seul su de ses nuages
place vide au cœur de soleil
qui fait ployer toutes les cordes

        du haut de mes yeux
d'où je ne vois rien tout à fait
du haut de mes yeux qui voient
        comme j'ai rêvé.

You wriggle and break
bird you wriggle and break

fooled by the fronds
known only by its clouds
hole in the heart of the sun
which bends all the strings

        from the tops of my eyes
where I see nothing at all
from the tops of my eyes which see
        as I had dreamed.

Irai-je cheminer
à la tête de foi
ou à l'himalaya.

Beau cet ange
tenant le soleil plat
le capricorne mange.

Les saintes savent bien courir
partout pleurantes chancelantes
et jolies rien ne mord ces anges

et les ancêtres naturels
levés sur les prairies de miel
au bord du ciel les tiges se croient sages.

Toute la nuit des mains ont agité les pages
aux flambeaux de cire de vin
le ciel la brandissait au poing
ton sourire sous les joues
porte de givre
porte d'épices toi qui manques.

Shall I march
to the peak of faith
or to the Himalayas.

Beautiful this angel
holding the sun flat
the capricorn eats.

The saints know well to run
everywhere tearful teetering
and charming nothing bites these angels

and ancestral elementals
awakened over fields of honey
at the edge of the sky the stalks feel wise.

All night hands waved the pages
to torches of wax of wine
the sky raises in its fist
your smile beneath the cheeks
gate of frost
gate of spice you who lack.

Il faut autre chose
des coraux des lampes partout
au velours fendu suspendues

comme des joncs creux a suivi mes bras
une moëlle au ciel d'ores et déjà.

Priées toutes aux coins se sont trouvées
le toucher rassemblait des bagues à tâtons
le bras se lève
prise la sève
de grands genoux et les échelles s'accomplissent
croyant à peine les degrés à la rencontre
si sûr là-haut voilà le fleuve
noir féminin comme marie.

Something else is needed
corals lamps abound
hung from split velvet

like hollow bangles following my arms
a marrow already in heaven.

All who prayed in the corners were found
rings joining together by touch
the arm rises
prizes the sap
large knees and the ladders manifest
barely believing the degrees of the encounter
so sure up there the river
dark feminine like mary.

Sur des ondes des plumes
toutes et toutes belles
expertes en horizon
aux fêtes panachées
oiseau tu hantes et brilles

es-tu cœur es-tu feu.

Dites-le-moi tous les rinceaux se balançaient
le vent d'adieu sonnait aux roses
dites-le-moi au coin vert du salon
les yeux les seins solaires le soleil
chez eux pour toujours pour personne.

Le parc dans la glace
le rêve laissé
qui pendait encore
festonnés de rideaux d'averses de couronnes
de hautes poussières
ce qu'on a en tête
aux pieds des verdures des cires
ce que les yeux soumettent.

Et toi, dans ces roues
doué de beau matin
doué de sud de nord
oiseau tu hantes et brilles.

Atop the waves are feathers
totality and total grace
experts on the horizon
in the motley celebrations
bird you haunt and glitter

are you heart are you fire.

Tell me all the rinceau was rocking
the farewell wind ringing the roses
tell me in the green corner of the room
solar breasts the eyes the sun
home forever for no one.

The park in the mirror
the abandoned dream
still hanging
decorated with curtains of showers of crowns
of lofty dust
what we have in mind
at the feet of greeneries and waxes
this that the eyes subject.

And you, in these wheels
endowed with beautiful morning
endowed with south and north
bird you haunt and glitter.

OÙ ES-TU TOI qui recommences
tes cheveux comme un bouquet
tenant les boules et les coupes.

La fleur de soleil penchait
je te tendis les guides vertes
et tu sautas au seul cœur qu'il fallait
sans tourner sans hésiter
sans te tromper
sans bouger

au milieu du sang de la lumière.

WHERE ARE YOU, you who begin again
your hair like a bouquet
keeping the balls and the cups.

Craning sunflower
I handed you the green reins
and you leaped into the only heart you needed
without turning without hesitating
without error
without moving

amidst the blood of the light.

Pour deux beaux yeux brillant de nuit à mon côté
après la bouche les dents
et le mur après l'élan
seuls égaux ces grands parents
d'après la nuit c'est le jour.

For two beautiful nocturnal eyes by my side
the teeth behind the lip
the wall behind the urge
equal only to those great relations
for behind the night is day.

Mes bêtes capricieuses revenaient des champs
criant pour venir partant sans rien dire
et toi tirant des bouts de chaînes
dans des herbes pleurant riant.

Ce fut la grande pureté
dans le jardin à le serrure
du corridor émerveillé.
Fraîche verveine fraîche
debout partout avec la nuit au bout.

My capricious beasts were returning from the fields
crying to come leaving without a word
and you pulling at the ends of the chains
in the grass crying laughing.

It was great purity
in the padlocked garden
of the spellbound corridor.
Fresh verbena fresh
stands high far and wide with night at the end.

QUE TIRAIT LE voile jeté
où pour la vie s'agrippaient tant d'insectes
et des armes à deux tranchants traînées.

À l'abri de bois emportés
à la nuit de lumières percée
plus noire que mon asile
à la neige au bois
à la bête au chien
le vent a seuls respecté du ciel les signes.

Pour vous en mars une couronne légère
pour vous en mars une couronne qui pèsera
alors que vous serez vécue
plus de fleurs et de branches
de branches de pluie
de tout plus que de votre sang.

What drew the tossed veil
where so many insects hung on for life
lugging double-edged swords behind them.

In the shelter of woods carried
to the night pierced by lights
darker than my sanctum
to the snow to the woods
to the beast to the dog
the wind only heeded signs from the sky.

For you in March a light crown
for you in March a crown that will weigh
whereas you will have experienced
more flowers and more branches
of branches of rain
of everything more than of your blood.

Par tant de portes
par ces génies symétriques comme les gémeaux
par les deux ailes
les litanies des tours
des bêtes et des herbes
et celles différentes des fenêtres
si belles revenant au même.

Plus je mourais moins je tenais mes promesses
plus je mourais plus il restait de pierres
les bras se fanaient
les tentures à la lune ne touchaient plus terre
plus je mourais plus la joie était lisse.

Condamnés à tout comme le papillon couleur de neige
complaisant à tirer la traîne de fiancé
à porter tendrement d'un jour à l'autre été
sa charge d'yeux de sable
te connaissant déjà certaine grande entière
ton doigt de verre meut le lierre
par les feuilles
par les branches
c'est passé.

Qui suit le courant qui fait le serment
après le mur éclate en étamines
est feu est terre fleur du ciel.

THROUGH SO MANY doors
through these genies and their gemini symmetry
by these two wings
the litanies of towers
of the beasts and the herbs
and those differing from windows
so beautiful coming back to the same.

The more I died the less I kept my promises
the more I died the more stones remained
the arms withered away
the moon's drapes no longer touched the earth
the more I died the more joy was leveled.

Condemned to it all like the snow-colored butterfly
delighted to drag the bridal train
to tenderly carry summer from one day to the other
its sandy-eyed burden
already knowing you certain vast whole
your glass finger moved the ivy
through the leaves
through the branches
it went.

Who follows the current who takes the oath
after the wall splits with stamens
becomes fire becomes earth flower of heaven.

Lointaine la branche à travers tirait forte comme une marée et doucement ce fut la folle à fleurs.

DISTANT THE BOUGH pulled fierce like a tide
and gently it was the madwoman of flowers.

Par des fronts de chevaux
par des fronts de croissants
et par des fronts de temps

et les cristaux ont sonné loin et plus encore.
Entre mon astre et moi la petite distance
la plus petite entre les yeux ouverts les yeux fermés
pourtant m'étant faite verte
je n'ai pu close à l'étoile
je n'ai pu fermer les yeux.

THROUGH VANGUARDS OF horses
through brows of crescents
through the fronts of time

and the crystals rang far and farther still.
Between my star and me a short distance
as short as that between eyes open and closed
yet having gone green
I could not enclose the star
I could not close my eyes.

Ô DAME DES pays
là sous le ciel et ce n'est pas peu dire
à regarder sous l'aile
entre l'aile et son ombre
à midi quand l'étoile
et moi brûlons la même vie
avec des signes
moi d'avance
elle parfois avec sa longue différence.

Tout enchanté de longtemps
le cœur dans sa grotte pend.

O LADY OF lands
there under heaven it is no trivial thing
to look beneath the wing
between the wing and its shadow
at noon when the star
and I burn the same life
with symbols
me ahead
she occasionally with her enduring difference.

All enchanted and for all time
the heart in its grotto hangs.

Quelle est cette seule compagnie mon sang qui coule
c'est mon sang qui coule et au-dedans luit
c'est la nuit dans laquelle le sang coule.

Et les signes les mains de l'air reviennent
tirant chacun son homme
les bras au corps dormants
engainé de longtemps.

Croix se déplie
et tourne roue
fleur se déplie
et tous arrivent seul[s].

WHAT IS THIS lone company my blood that flows
it is my blood that flows and glows within
it is the night into which blood flows.

And the symbols the hands return from the air
each pulling its man
arms sleeping on bodies
sheathed forever.

    Cross unfolds
    and wheel spins
    flower unfolds
    and all arrive[s] alone.

TOUTES LES SORCELLERIES
tombèrent comme les pierres dans le puits
tu aimas et ce fut mai.

La folle traînait les champs
d'herbes et de cheveux
qui dormant l'un dans l'autre en mai
la folle courait les yeux.
Réveillé de la terre
ton cœur dans ton fief
tes mains loin
ces buissons de clôture avec un nid chacune.

Coupés les lauriers c'est l'étang de sel
les lanières
c'est la fleur dépouillée de jéricho brûlé
deux tisons en croix c'est la flamme
la béante la suffisante
la mère bombée
géante des dos des poitrines
aux oreilles de feuilles.

Entre mes mains qui arrivaient douces voici l'offrande
mes mains ont brûlé
ma tête bonne un creux des genoux plus de tête
la bête si intense à la bête plus de bête.

Je te fais le serment d'à présent sans manies
le oui sans paupières
le serment d'eau sans bords

du moule du dernier cœur
la fleur sans franges
l'homme sans terres.

THE WHOLE OF witchcraft
fell into the well like a stone
you loved and it was May.

The madwoman lingered in the fields
of herbs and hair
one sleeping within the other in May
the madwoman's eyes roamed.
Awoken from the earth
your heart in your fief
your hands beyond
such enclosing shrubs with one nest each.

Trim the laurels this is the salt pond
the ribbons
the flowers stripped by Jericho's blaze
two crosswise embers this is the flame
the gaping the adequate
the swollen mother
giant of back and bosom
with ears of leaves.

Between my gently drawn hands the offering
my hands burned
my fine head a nook between knees no more head
the beast so ferociously the beast no more beast.

I vow to you now without compulsion
the open-eyed I do
the boundless oath of water

    from the mold of the final heart
    the flower reduced to stem
    the man without land.

La boule n'a plus de coupe dors
les valets sont tombés les uns sur les autres dors
les couleurs sont rentrées sous les ailes dors

par la porte des cendres
les feux menaient au feu.

The ball no longer with the cup, sleep.
The servants fallen atop each other, sleep.
The colors withdrawn under the wings, sleep

through the ash door
fires leading to fire.

Je faisais la roue
par des étamines
des doigts de lumière
une expiration qui ne revenait plus
d'aucuns parages
et tant de coraux fleurissaient mon eau
en quel pays croire.

Au poing fermé à la médaille dans le poing
de plomb de gris
au précipice de brûlure
et de neige se détestant
où roulent en se mordant
les frères nés de longtemps.

Au bord sans plumes
au bord sans peau
ma sœur belle à l'abri me regardait tomber
et je riais en elle.

I CARTWHEELED
through stamens
fingers of light
an exhalation which no longer returned
from anywhere near
and so many corals decorated my water
in which country to believe.

The fist clenched and the medallion within
lead grey
on the precipice of burns
and snow loathing itself
where rolling around biting one another
the brothers born of the ages.

Featherless on the edge
skinless on the edge
my beautifully sheltered sister watched me fall
and I laughed within her.

Mon mince mon haut lion
partait chevauché au bout des ornières
libre des yeux libre des dents
comme un seul grand homme de joie
un homme de ciel
le ciel en face du visage
jouant à midi aux étoiles
à l'eau des puits de nuit
criant rayons à foison.

Sans secret de pierre et feuilles
le père vert et la mère
de gages de voix d'ailes et de soie
la dame de tout là-haut dans sa joie.
Ni eau ni lune
ni vieil arbre de paille et autre aurore
la tête entre les mains du grand seigneur secouait ses larmes
l'ormeau tremblait comme une bête précieuse

et dans ses chansons comme des abeilles
au royaume d'est de miel
la roue sur les yeux et doux le soleil
pas usé non décroisé
n'était pas né le chanteur.

My thin my lofty lion
rode off to the ditches' end
free of eyes free of teeth
like a single great man of joy
a man of the sky
the sky in front of your face
playing at noon to the stars
to the water of wells of night
crying beams prolifically.

Without secret of stone and leaf
the green father and mother
of pledges of voice of wings and of silk
the lady of all up above in her joy.
Neither water nor moon
nor old tree of straw and other aurora
the head between the great master's hands shaking its tears
the elm trembles like a precious beast

and in her songs like bees
in the kingdom east of honey
the wheel on the eyes and sweet the sun
neither used nor crossed
the singer yet unborn.

Elle a dit la cubaine
en poussant son ombrelle
si seule est la bête.

S'est émietté l'oiseau de pierre
dans des sauts des carrés nouveaux
nous irons tous aux bois si beaux soient-ils
avec des traînes de pierre.

AND SHE SAID the Cubana
while opening her umbrella
so lonesome is the beast.

The bird of stone falls to pieces
in leaps from new squares
we will all go to the woods beautiful as they are
wearing trains of stone.

En butte à deux vagues
errants du matin
c'est aujourd'hui la chasse
du blanc orné sur le noir seul

aux fleuves de proie
nous avons toujours navigué
et les mains en rond
aux balcons ouverts
à tout trembler sur de tels bords.

Le nuage vert connu et de sumac de la douleur
qui amplifie sa forêt
bien loin après se partage et se sourit
d'une bouche de feuilles nouvelles

autour du feu de mots
il fait beau et beau et jour
dans le crochet du milieu
la bouche a parlé le jour.

Confronting two waves
wanderers of the morning
today the hunt
of the ornate white over the simple black

atop rivers of prey
we have always sailed
and the circle of our hands
on the open balconies
shaking everything over such edges.

Familiar green clouds and sorrow's sumac
elevates the forest
well after splitting and smiling
with a mouth of new leaves

around the fire of words
it is pleasant and beautiful and daytime
in the crook of the milieu
the mouth had spoken the day.

Je viens ma mère grave de pierre
ou si tu souris de coquillages
je viens ô entrée sous ta paille
manteau de feuilles
arbre assistant
planche des masques.

Pieds sans jupe à tes seins ne pendent que des trous
ne cache rien et tu dis tout
vierge avec toutes ses raisons
souveraine du luisant
voilà la nuit de la traîne.

Seule comme la voûte et la coquille,
pour personne et pour rien en vérité
ciel des chênes
plus que jamais
à vue à vie à mort la place est gardée.

I AM COMING O mother solemn as stone
or if you smile with seashells
I come invited under your straw
coat of leaves
supportive tree
board of masks.

Skirtless feet only holes hang from your breasts
hiding nothing you say it all
virgin with all her reasons
sovereign of the glimmer
alas the night of the bridal train.

Alone like the vault and the shell
truly for no one and for nothing
sky of oaks
more than ever
by sight in life in death the space is guarded.

Fleuris douce
rêve souple admirant tes étamines
pour toi je connais l'écorce et le clou.

Noire j'écoute ta graine
de pavot blanc
et non pour que oui revienne
et nuit pour que jour retourne.

Première chassant l'autre
mauvaise parfaite
tuant au soupçon
première sans tort
qui piétine ce qu'on apporte et puis qui dort
pâle contre toute la terre
jument dans son droit
tu penches sur moi de plus en plus large
tu ris de mes raisons
tu ris de ma verdure
à tâtons rien ne m'est laissé
tu descends le degré d'avant
distance
avant blanche
robe qui brûle.

Sweet bloom
supple dream admiring your stems
for you I come to know the bark and the nail.

Black I listen to your white
poppy seed
and no so that yes returns
and night so that day returns.

First hunting the other
perfect wretch
killing out of suspicion
first without error
tramples what we bring and then sleeps
pale against all the land
mare in her right
you lean over me larger and larger
you laugh at my reasons
you laugh at my lush verdancy
fumbling blindly nothing is left of me
you descend the degree ahead
distance
whiteness ahead
dress of fire.

Au grenier en tête
la si belle tour
grises grises les souris
l'arbre pendait sans le fruit.

L'herbe à la lune la plante souveraine que dis-tu d'elle
que je suis d'ici
il m'en semble ce qui me ressemble
passé par son miel de graines
venu de pluie sans fronton
de main racines tirées
dans les rideaux de tout belle accouchée.

Sans lumière était venu
au grenier a dit venu
allumé halluciné
qui brûla comme village.

La terre l'eau ont soif qui s'ennuient
une bête de dieu vit à fendre l'âme
le gant de pierre baisé de la vierge
se repose amoureux sur les épaules de la sève.
Baignés dormons dans les cheveux et les sourires
des morceaux aveugles comme des baisers
avec quoi m'aimes-tu m'oublies
avec endroit envers de feuille
et les poignées ne seront plus qu'étoiles
et la soie s'est assise au ciel a souri et tout est dit.

In the attic in the head
the tower so beautiful
brown brown the mouse
the tree suspended without fruit.

Moon grass sovereign plant what do you say of her
that I am from here
it seems what resembles me
passed through its seeded honey
came from the rain with no gables
from hand pulled roots
into the curtains of every beautiful new mother.

Without light it came
into the attic it spoke came
kindled dazzled
burned like village.

The earth the water are thirsty grow bored
a beast of god lives in heartbreak
the kissed stone glove of the virgin
resting lovingly on shoulders of sap.
Bathed we sleep in the hair and the smiles
blind morsels like kisses
with what do you love me forget me
with the front and back of a leaf
the handles will no longer be mere stars
the silk took a seat in the sky smiled and all was said.

Poèmes
(1937)

Poems

À Une Femme À Une Route

Ce corps ici féminin qui pend comme une
    goutte lointaine
vers l'autre ici cette fois féminin
où les cheveux égaux en travers le sourire
        folle fuseau
        pointus les os
qui traversera des plaines avec ses hanches
qui brassera la paille pas des langes il dormira
    aux granges
seul pour les herbes
dont l'amie ne se soucia jamais quoique verte
par destin par grain par chemin par satin
lames de feuilles ses yeux plats clous dans le
    bois
à la forêt toutes ses dents
rocher doux crâne de fougères
si grande je l'ai tirée cette née
comme un troupeau d'eau
accroché aux falaises
aux steppes quand on la croit aux fraises
avec des rubans sauvages au lieu de dormir
du côté total vert et rouge.

La belle la châtaine
ma souris marron que tu es loin sous les
    buissons

Prise de seins de mains et de cheveux
jamais sortie tout entière elle-même
si folle de lichens perdue
comme une aiguille dans la mousse

For A Woman For A Road

This body here feminine hangs like a
        distant droplet
toward the other here feminine this time
where hair even across the smile
                mad spindle
                sharpened bones
she will cross plains with her hips
she will beat the straw not the swaddle she will sleep
        in the granges
alone for the herbs
for whom the friend will never worry however green
by destiny by grain by path by satin
blades of leaves her flat eyes nails in the
        wood
in the forest all her teeth
soft rock skull of fern
so vast I drew forth this birth
like a flock of water
hung from the cliffs
on the steppes when one believes her at the strawberries
with wild ribbons instead of sleep
on the whole side green and red.

Brunette beauty
my brown mouse how far under those
        shrubs you are

Seized by breasts by hands by hair
never released entirely herself
so mad over lost lichens
like a needle in the moss

par tous les bouts urgente fausse
je t'ai tournée tu m'as tissée

Ta cave importait comme des montagnes
où l'ardoise chemine
où il pleut fait soleil le diable bat ses filles
où la faucille à fendre l'or habite et siffle,

Blessée indifférente laisse crier sa tête,
les mains dans les besognes
et le corps repoussé si doux pourtant sans tête
caressé de ses mains à d'autres horizons.

Velours chanson dans la cuirasse
l'étouffée pour rire
petite aux naseaux des montagnes
jouait avec les ânes.

À présent dormons sur des bras de neige
en fin de temps te voilà étendue
si je te pense chaude à longueur de désert
natte à refaire sous les palmes
forêt dans tes beaux jours
tout gorge de tour
élastique comme le renard des rêves
dure comme ton poing
revenue à ta plus simple expression
                                    d'être tout

by all the ends urgent false
I spun you you wove me

Your cave moves like mountains
where the slate advances
where it rains sun shines the devil beats his daughters
where the gold cleaving sickle lives and whistles

Wounded indifferent allows her head to cry
hands in the toil
and the body grown back so soft however headless
caressed by her hands to other horizons.

Velvet song in the breastplate
she snuffed it for a laugh
small in the nares of impasses
playing with the asses.

At present we sleep in arms of snow
at the end of time there you expand
if I think you hot to desert lengths
braids to plait once again under the palms
forest in your beautiful days
all full of towers
elastic like the oneiric fox
tough like your fist
brought once more to your simplest expression
of total being

GRAND VISAGE DE roche et d'herbe
si noir montré que je ne crains plus.
Te voir tu m'as sortie du puits d'un coup de cils
sans fond du lac où le soleil était le même
même le chêne noir des meubles de l'hiver
les recoins de maison laissée au carrefour
les flèches étaient fausses
bleues de poison mentaient

Pont de terre
viens qu'on te casse
au milieu où l'on passe
tour de terre où ton roi ne tient pas à toi
où le troupeau s'engouffre
tandis qu'hors de sa peau jaune obscure une route
large comme une femme
les pieds en avant
se chauffant au bout du monde
la plus incertaine
sans pattes de velours
allant aux panthères
tandis que cette route
sans têtes d'hommes
se porte comme une tête.

Sur un talus doux et roux la camomille
face au salon plein de l'amour des jeunes filles
à l'ouest d'écuelle de châtaignier pour les châtaignes
où le bois luit coupé vif se dentelle
les fleurs révélées tournent et éclairent
la mule au bois sonne comme une colonie
la douce sans retour au jardin des dahlias
                                        masquée de mauve
                                        plante sauve
tes dents de lapin tu n'y peux plus rien.

GREAT FACE OF rock and herb
shown so dark that I am no longer afraid.
Seeing you you released me from the wells in the blink of an eye
without bottom from the lake where the sun was the same
even the black oak of winter's furnishings
the house's recesses placed at the crossroads
the arrows were fake
poison's blues deceived

Earthen bridge
come let us break you
in the place where we pass
the tower of earth where your king has no hold over you
where the herd stampedes
while outside its yellow skin a road is obscured
wide as a woman
feet forward
warming herself at the end of the world
the most uncertain
without velvet paws
going to the panthers
even as this road
without human heads
proceeds like a head.

On a subdued maroon embankment the chamomile
faces a room full of the love of young girls
in the west a chestnutwood porringer for the chestnuts
where the wood shines freshly cut self-serrated
revealed flowers revolve and illuminate
the mule in the woods sounds off like a colony
the gentle one exiled to the dahlias
                        masked with mallow
                        hallow plant
your protruding teeth nothing can be done.

Sur un air indien
tenant mon tablier
cueilli mes têtes coupées
sainte germaine d'europe
pieds nus dans les petites euphorbes
comme des tuiles plu dessus au nord
comme des vaches embrassant partout
comme un chapelet autour du cou
me voilà tout
me voilà finie
me voilà nouée
me voilà rejointe
cous coupés je danse comme un oiseau
la fontaine hors du crâne

S'ébattant de rayons
il roule à volonté ce grand cœur meublé sur la route
douce comme rien
bordée de moules creux
frégate du soleil
sur cette retrouvée
dont la moelle jadis arcboutée au plafond avec son ombre
augurait les festins des blanches belettes
de l'éblouissement.

To an Indian tune
holding my pinafore
harvesting severed heads
saint germaine of Europe
barefoot in the tiny euphorbias
like tiles rained down in the north
like cows kissing everywhere
like a rosary around the neck
here I am all
here I am complete
here I am fashioned
here I am adjoined
necks gashed I dance like a bird
the fountain beyond the skull

Frolicking in fractals
it rolls at will this great heart set upon the road
sweet as nothing
lined with hollow molds
warship of the sun
on this discovery
whose marrow once braced the ceiling with its shadow
heralding the banquets of white weasels
of wonder.

Le cœur de tous les soirs l'oiseau d'eau est près de l'eau
faible papillon chante pour s'entendre
faible papillon petite la femme
petites ses mains posées comme ignorante
sur les jouets de la flamme

Qui monte et qui monte
aux himalayas
l'échelle de soie
à nouveau sortie
brillait dans la cave

L'échelle la hache le feu l'étincelle
tout a éclaté de rire de plus belle
la première fleur a dansé
une autre dame elle est partie
les navires sont détachés.
Adieu adieu le vœu des bêtes de mousson
le rat qui piaule noir et les yeux de lanternes
et toi magicienne qui mâche
des brins de cristal herbe à l'ombre loin au revoir
les pieds d'argile n'avançaient pas sous tes statues
les seins froids hors du parc souviens-toi de ce vent
boudeur et dédaignant hors mesure les palmes.

J'ai dormi dans un lit
de bambous et de nids
quand le soleil d'hiver
fend en deux l'opaline.

THE HEART OF all evenings the waterbird near its water
weak butterfly sings to hear itself
weak butterfly little the wife
her small hands resting as if ignorant
on the toys of the flame

Which rises and rises
up to the Himalayas
the ladder of silk
brought out once more
glimmered within the cave

The ladder the axe the fire the spark
everything erupted in most sonorous laughter
the first flower danced
another woman she left
ships unmoored.
Farewell farewell the vow of monsoon beasts
the rat chirping dark and lantern eyes
and you stuttering sorceress
crystal sprigs shadow herb distant goodbye
the clay feet do not advance beneath your statues
the cold breasts outside the grounds do you recall this wind
immeasurably sullen and loathing the palms.

I slept in a bed
of bamboo and nests
when winter's sun
split opaline in two.

SI JE N'EN sors pas dans l'or j'en mourrai
cette bête tenant mes rêves aux narines
la voilà d'hôpital et la voilà de cloches
et si je dois subir sa peau striée de pluie
adieu je suis à l'extrémité de mes fleuves.

Dans la boue du bengale aux doux noms de rosiers
et des coromandels flairés par les moustiques
je n'ai pas décoché cet ultime navire
le dernier pavillon et le trésor expirent

        Fière fière et dense
        suis la boule en flammes
        qui court les étages
        des hôtels du rêve.
        Il y a des danses
        de pâte et de lune
pour la fille seule par-dessus les toits
        la reine travaille

Tu iras danser au malabar
avec des joues de cuivre
avec le soleil aisé
avec du monde
plus seule avec le moustique
les papillons nouveaux seront donnés de race sûre
sur le poing les lumières du temps offertes
cœur de tous les soirs faible papillon oiseau
d'eau près de l'eau
faible papillon chante pour s'entendre.

If I don't come out in gold it will kill me
that beast holding my dreams in its nostrils
here she is from hospital and here she is from bells
and if I must suffer her rain-streaked skin
farewell I am at the limit of my rivers.

In the Bengal mud with sweet rose names
and the coromandel sought by the mosquitos
I did not dispatch that final ship
the last flag and the treasure expired

        Proud proud and dense
        follow the flaming ball
        which runs each floor
        of hotels of dreams.
        There are dances
        of pastry and of moon
for the daughter alone up over the rooftops
        the queen labors.

You will dance in Malabar
with copper cheeks
with the prosperous sun
with the crowd
no longer alone with the mosquito
the fresh butterflies will be delivered from a sure breed
over the fist the gifted lights of time
heart of all evenings weak butterfly wading
bird near the water
weak butterfly sings to hear itself.

Tête de mon corps
il fait soleil
c'est le jour de la pierre levée
c'est le jour de passer entre les fleurs
et deux enfants tombant d'extase tout le temps
nos feux dans le bon vent
que dieu nous garde dans la poussière et près de la mangue
l'esprit du trésor l'or le voleur est dans l'arbre
adieu passant
adieu pour la nuit mon aimée
l'auberge de la senteur blanche me gardera
vous êtes loin ma tête d'ombrelles de fête
ma tige de soie prosternée
et cependant ton lit plein de lin bleu restait aux branches
c'était autrefois les jolies les doubles
ô mon bel étang
mille papillons blancs brûlant
sortaient de raison suffisante
par-dessus l'épaule d'étoile
pas large long le sillon
elle était au bout
avec un grillon.

Maintenant le vent de mousson qui ne fait pas l'ascète
et l'araignée pendant le plus clair de son temps
couronne d'huile et d'or le char tiré par les serpents et par
[les pierres
c'est ma couleur
de voir sur la vie.

La lune entre les cornes
à bombay de port à bombay de mouches
dieu entre les cornes
j'ai ce poids sur moi

—

Head of my body
the shining sun
it is the day for the lifted stone
the day to pass between the flowers
and two children fall ecstatic without end
our fires in the sweet wind
let god protect in the dust and near the mango
the essence of treasure the gold the thief is in the tree
a passing farewell
farewell for the night my beloved
the hostel of white fragrance shields me
you are far away my head from festive parasols
my prostrated silken stalk
yet your bed full of blue linen remains in the branches
it once was the darlings and the doubles
o my precious pool
one thousand white butterflies burning
abandoning sufficient reason
beyond the star's shoulder
not large long the indent
she was at the end
with a cricket.

Now monsoon wind which does not abstain
and the spider during the clearest of weather
crown of oil and gold the chariot pulled by serpents and stones
this is the color
with which I look upon life.

The moon between the horns
to Bombay of port to Bombay of flies
I have this weight atop me

C'est une vérité dans le bec de la colombe
l'arbre des fées est dans le front y restera
haute vivante ne tremblera plus d'amour
peau de cheval près du gui tremblera.

Prend la fleur sourit la jette
à quoi servait ce soleil
le côté du retour est gauche et noir
il reçoit le contraire d'avoir aimé
le contraire d'avoir tissé
il reçoit la queue de requin
tête tournée prend les baisers
un autre cœur plus vrai te tire
là où tombent les horizons
où bas les chevaux de terre attendent
adieu ma fleur et ma forêt.

Tout perdu jardin gagné d'ombre
sans oiseaux sans parfums
tête de mon corps mes yeux il fait soleil.

This is a truth in the beak of the dove
the faerie tree is there in the front where it will remain
those that live high will no longer tremble with love
beneath mistletoe horse hide will quiver.

                    Take the flower smile toss it aside
                    to what end this sun
the side of the return is left and black
it receives the opposite of having loved
the opposite of having woven
it receives the shark's tail
the turned head catches the kisses
another heart more true draws you in
there where horizons fall
down where the horses of the earth await
                    farewell my flower and my forest.

All is lost the garden seized with shadow
without birds without essence
head of my body my eyes the shining sun.

Le dernier jour qui détruit le soleil je brûle
derrière mon lit creux d'amandes vertes
d'une frénésie de cris de souris
ma voile de dieu me voilà partie

La rose d'automne a prié pour nous
c'est un chant d'ancêtre à travers la pluie
mais la dalle douce n'a pas tenu
mon pas traversant aux mers alliées.
Vers cet échafaud de fruits murmurés
je pends comme un lis
ou piétine loin
sous feuilles d'antan.

Quand frottée de santal
mon trésor mon amour
la lèvre du beau jour.
Que croit ta voix miracle sans nocturne
la lèvre languit la paupière se troue
on chante des psaumes de pauvres en effet
mais pour les vallées dont le ciel se remue tendre
jamais assez parlé d'une langue de feuilles

Ce miel bref il est parti avec la fuyante
au détour d'une allée une mousse a tourné
ah qui me donnera debout et triste et blanche
et pure sous ses yeux les mains croisées de l'ange
mille batailles ont glissé sous les délices
lointains d'anciens oiseaux à l'horizon des branches
partez loin roses et ces tiges féminines
ces langueurs et les gorges trop âpres pour vivre
mais les roseaux franchis comme un blessé couchée
aux cuvettes du ciel et le seul poids des lièvres
pure petite bouche de goujon au ruisseau terne

THE LAST DAY which destroyed the sun I burn
behind my bed hollow with green almonds
with a wildness of cries of mice
my veil of god thus left me

The autumn rose prayed for us
an ancestral song all through the rain
but the soft flagstone did not hold
my step crossing into allied waters.
Toward that gallows of mumbled fruit
I dangle like a lily
or stumble far
below the leaves of yesteryear.

Scrubbed with santal
my treasure my love
the lip of a beautiful day.
What your voice believes miracle without nocturne
the lip shrivels the lid perforates
we sing psalms of the poor in fact
but for the valleys that the skies softly stir
never enough spoken of a language of leaves

This brief honey went with the vanishing point
round the bend of an alley a moss turned
ah who will give me upright and sad and white
and pure in its eyes the angel's clasped hands
a thousand battles slipped under the pleasures
distant ancient birds on the horizon of branches
go far away roses and these feminine stems
these languors and the throats too cruel for life
but the reeds broken through as if a wounded man
in the basin of the sky and the sole weight of hares
pure little gudgeon mouth lying in the lifeless brook

j'ai dit la mort des points d'or la jappeuse
de noms de fleurs ah qu'elle est dure l'orpheline

Lierre a tourné
feuilles d'acier
bleu est rentré
dans sa mère pour longtemps

Je dors dans le nid
l'herbe l'épée montent la garde
les voix deviennent mon abri
le blanc le rouge s'y regardent
ailleurs c'était le parc de rien
venez ma vivante

I spoke the death of golden stitches the groaner
of flower names ah how tough she is the orphan

Ivy has turned
leaves of steel
blue has gone back
into its mother forever

I sleep in the nest
the grass and the sword mount the guard
the voices become my refuge
the white the red look there
elsewhere it was the garden of nothing
come along my living one

ON DISAIT FORT je porte ta tour dans ma bouche
pesant du poids de ta vie d'ivoire et sans ronces
on disait bas ce qui se noie
la chose l'île à fond de planète.

Sans joie
lourde la tour qui est là
avec le bonheur de son peu de joie
des artifices d'or s'en échappent encor
tandis que chevelure a d'entières ténèbres
et la forêt que j'ai rêvée.

Il n'y a plus de nuit tout est blanc tout étale
non revenus d'antiques étendues ou nous fait mal pourtant
les mains brûlent dehors les campagnes gémissent
tombées à ce cristal qui de nous n'était pas
ce n'était que l'une après l'autre la bouche et la coupe
des averses rouges passaient entre les ciels
une main si aveugle alors touchait des fleurs
que la nuit de l'enfance avait connu bombées

Il y eut bien des ailes
d'abeilles en vérité
et même à l'autre bout de l'enfer des charmilles
et des pistils de lis au long du jour sucés
par les bêtes sorties sans hâte

Quoi donc est fait ainsi de poussière et de craie
où les trèfles étaient
à quel âge à quels bords de pierre
tour de l'amour la pesante la légère
c'était trop comme une éphémère à mourir
épaulée au cylindre et des sanglots des cheveux aux hanches
avec des fièvres assez belles pourtant
éclatée comme un rêve des dernières cendres.

Loudly they said I carry your tower in my mouth
balancing the weight your ivory life without bramble
said down low is what drowns
the thing the island at planet's end.

Without joy
heavy that tower there
with the fortune of its hint of joy
golden artifices evade it once more
whilst hair is dressed with complete darkness
and the forest I have dreamt.

There is no longer night everything is white all is still
not returned from ancient expanses or hurting us nonetheless
the hands burn beyond the moaning fields
fallen upon this crystal which came not from us
it was but one after the other the mouth and the cup
red torrents passing between the skies
the one hand so blind then touched flowers
that the night of childhood had seen protruding.

There were many wings
of bees indeed
and even at the other end of the inferno arbors
and pistils of lilies suckled the day long
by listless tarrying beasts

What thus is made from powder and limestone
where the clovers were
at what age at which stone borders
tower of love the heavy the light
too much like a mayfly to die
shouldered to the cylinder and tears from hair to hips
with fevers pretty enough all the same
scattered like a dream of final ashes.

Eau je te veux
et plante et feu
chair dit-elle tour clairvoyante

Et la tour qui durait durait comme toujours
emportée dans les feux de la bouche
absente inaliénée
ton visage n'a pas tourné
ne s'est ouvert ni s'est fermé
seule tu vois le jour
sur maux sur ambres et sur flots
signée après le sang
sur les feux malmenés ton poids d'os et de cœur
ivoire le dernier os de monde.

Water I want you
and plant and fire
flesh said she clairvoyant tower

And the tower which endured endured like always
carried off in the fires of the mouth
absent inalienated
your face does not turn
neither open nor closed
alone you see the day
over evils ambers and waves
signed after the blood
over mangled fires your burdens of bones and heart
ivory the last bone of the world.

À Francesca

Mains doux myosotis aux crosses des fusils
je lutte je suis prosternée
après les morts dans tes cheveux comme des faux
toi chanteuse des os profonds des soldats des matelots

For Francesca

Hands sweet forget-me-not dress the stocks of rifles
I fight I am prostrate
after the dead like scythes in your hair
you singer of the depths of the bones of soldiers of sailors

Séville

Le vent propre lavait de tous les rendez-vous
par la porte et le loup
on reviendra Maria de Padilla
vers la mosquée sainte de ta mantille
mais le vent tel habite les rames du ciel.

Padilla
avec son pied chaussé
dans une résille
du temps où elle était

La cormorane aux plages des fleuves qui vont à la mer
le bec sous les tabacs les tuiles de l'allée
c'est l'olivier d'Espagne et nous irons laver
plus bas l'andalousie
qui dort belle la nuit
de bombes de tigres de têtes au collier
nous irons laver ces yeux bleus
qui nous ont plus tué que vous.

Seville

The clean wind washed the encounters from everyone
through the door and the wolf
we will come see you Maria de Padilla
towards the holy mosque of your mantilla
but wind as such inhabits the oars of the sky.

Padilla
her foot taken
in a fishnet
from whence she had been

the cormorant on the sands of rivers flowing to the sea
the beak under the tobacco the tiles of the alley
this is the Spanish olive tree and we will go to wash
further below Andalusia
sleeping beautiful the night
of bombs of tigers of yoked heads
we will go to wash these blue eyes
which killed us more than you.

LE CORAIL DANS la main
le corail dans le sein
loin des pelouses heureuses de mon pays
les dames de la vie les étoiles tombent dans le puits
ô fortuné voyage
il sonne le temple le poney sauvage
j'ai laissé ta robe ô ma bien-aimée
accrochée au bas d'un arbre de mai

À présent avec mon poing
et ma lance
à présent avec ma vie
qui court dans les branches
l'ours sous la clématite de l'himalaya chante
la fenêtre est de nuit la femme saute au feu
le mince monastère au-delà de la frange
de bois studieux qui fument sous des tapis bleus

Les pied pleins de démons
ah ma pauvre violette
toi que j'ai tant aimée
où la mare me guette

De mes bras descendant des lances de vallée
je ne puis rien pour toi à ce puits de délices
la feuille y crie avec la lave et la sibylle.

Coral in my hand
coral within my breast
far from my country's joyous lawns
ladies of life the stars fall into the well
o bountiful voyage
sounds the temple the wild pony
o my beloved I left your dress
hanging on the trunk of a maypole

Now with my fist
and my lance
now with my life
that courses through the boughs
the bear sings underneath himalayan leatherflower
the window is made of night the woman leaps into fire
the frail monastery beyond the fringe
of studious woods which smolder beneath blue carpets

Feet full of demons
ah my poor violet
I have loved you so
where the ponds awaited me

From my arms lowering these valley lances
nought will be done for you in this well of delight
where the leaf cries out with molten rock and sybil.

Chère à t'aimer comme la marguerite qui s'éveille
pliée présente dans les givres noirs sans ailes
parfois morte portée au cou de talisman
tu cherches de tes bords la bonté de la terre
je prends dehors ta main la graine blanche belle

Comme tes seins sont des soleils voient sur ton corps
volons bouche de dame
volons ensemble
et dame vole loin.

Je nie entre nuit et jour à voix égale
à jamais l'amour qui ne butte
sur un astre fermé
le dire de toi
de tes pistils qui dépassent mes bras
des mauves où préside
ancrée à la fin de ce bouquet qui plie
cette taille amoureuse
sourire du donjon

Les rinceaux de ta chair retombent sur la dalle
l'animal aux carreaux et la violette enfouie
quand toute tige au nord est morte et que le cloître
soutient là-bas des fruits de salpêtre et de mangue
les yeux fermés de la fermée
allons sur ces barques
et puis sur ce fleuve
et ces yeux qui mentent
et ces cils d'étang

C'est la nuit de velours rouge les granges du tropique la
[mendiante mendie
le signe du battant l'orage acariâtre
là lutte cet oiseau lavé des mains de pluie

Dear to love you like the awakening daisy
pursed now and wingless in the black frost
sometimes dead carried in a talisman around the neck
you seek from your borders the bounty of the earth
I take your hand outside the beautiful white seed

Like your breasts are suns looking over your body
let's fly lady lips
let's fly together
and lady fly far.

I deny between night and day with even voice
eternally love does not stumble
upon a closed star
to say so of you
of your pistils slipping through my arms
from mallows where presides
anchored at the end of this bending bouquet
that amorous waistline
a smile from the dungeon

The scroll of your flesh falls once more onto the slab
the animal in the tiles and the burrowed violet
when every stalk in the north is dead and the cloister
supports from below fruits of saltpeter and mango
the closed eyes of the narrowly shut
let's board these ships
and then this river
and these eyes which deceive
and these pondside lashes

It is the night of red velvet the tropical granges the beggar
begged
the sign of the warrior the ill-tempered storm
there struggles that bird washed by hands of rain

si douce toi dedans aux vitres de ma course
parée abandonnée comme un siècle dernier

À l'embrasure de tes larmes
à ta semelle de soie quand là-bas la force des armes
à mon genêt d'Espagne
pomponné de niranes d'étoiles noires et de galanes.

so sweet you inside at the windows of my course
adorned abandoned like a previous century

To the doorway of your tears
to your tread of silk when down below the power of swords
to my bush of Spanish broom
primped with *niranes* of black stars and chelones.

Aux grands pieds la poule des joncs qui fend
        son pain auprès de l'eau
le royaume de l'écureuil qui chante haut
les peines de la lune les lourdes délivrées les célosies
elles c'est bien c'est pour ici mon jasmin
les poings des fleurs l'étoupe des jardins sur les yeux
honte de ne pas regarder aux fenêtres trouées
le bosquet des yeux
je le sais bien
je n'y peux rien
c'est le soleil

Et jamais de la vie en vie ne s'en délie.
Même en des rues petites les roses de jais s'obscurcissent
d'autres sont de crin d'or et d'autres à la bouche
l'amaranthe dont le nom et la grandeur étouffent la ville
les galanes de nuit
si douces c'est assez fortes sans travailler
en votre cœur sûres et de beauté tournez.

La fille étrangère
pleurait dans son lit
mais tu n'es plus elle
peut-être Mercure.

J'ai cherché les ponts sur Lerida
les talons trempaient puis montaient
on ne mange pas de ce pain-là
avec deux étoiles à la bouche.

WITH LARGE FEET the hen of bulrush cracks
        her bread beside the water
the kingdom of squirrels who belt out
the moon's sorrows the heaviness lifted from the coxcombs
they are good and fine for my jasmine here
the flowers' fists the gardens' tow over the eyes
shame to not peer through pierced windows
the copse of eyes
I know it well
I am helpless
against the sun

And never does life in living absolve it.
Even on small roads the onyx roses confound
others are of golden horsehair and others like mouths
the amaranth whose name and grandeur suffocates the town
evening's chelones
so gentle but effortlessly strong
in your hearts you spin steadfast with beauty.

The unknown girl
crying in her bed
you are no longer her
but Mercury perhaps.

I searched the bridges over Lleida
the heels dunked then brought up
we do not eat of that bread
with two stars on the lips.

Sorts de la lueur
(1937)

Spells of the Glimmer

Le loup tourne à la porte
l'oiseau tourne à la proue
à la campagne les revenants
merci compagnie.

Au bout du pont de fer voici les féminines
se glissant en pistils dans les veines de dieu
la plus blanche attelée à la mare est restée
béante du troupeau léger sans rien tâcher

Ouvre la bouche
ma fleur pour ne pas chanter.

Le vent prenant aux cheveux les fuseaux les narcisses
ton cœur dansant aux îles de jupons aussi d'oiseaux
comme un point cardinal ta main l'arrête et dresse
son miroir impérieux où l'on voit des bateaux

Pourtant si fière que possible ma marguerite
tu ne vaux pas l'arbre aux yeux d'amadou
la belle de mon bois magnifique attardée
y lovait chaque soir le velours de ses os

Sortant de son voyage aux surfaces fleuries
par-dessus les cols blancs et les anneaux tachés
ma ville fiancée aux portes harnachées
écoutait clouées à l'écorce les oreilles des sirènes
et le galop du vent dans ses voiles forés

C'est toi la vierge de la pierre dite
tes crins éparpillés servent ton centre étroit
et le soleil couché et le bateau sombré
n'en savent pas plus long que toi la non partie.

THE WOLF TURNS at the door
the bird turns at the bow
phantoms out in the country
thank you company.

Here at the end of the iron bridge are the feminines
slipping into pistils in the veins of god
bound to the pond the whitest remained
agape from the spritely band not sullying a thing

Open your mouth
my flower so as not to sing.

The wind taking in its hair the spindles and narcissus
your heart dancing in the islands of petticoats as well as of birds
like a cardinal point your hand stops it and lifts
your imperious mirror in which boats can be seen

While impossibly proud my daisy
you are not the tree with eyes of amadou
the lingering beauty of my magnificent woods
coiling there each night the velvet of its bones

Forsaking its journey to the floral surfaces
above the white necks and stained rings
my betrothed city with doors enchained
the siren's ears pricked pinned to the bark
and the gallop of the wind in its pierced sails

You are the virgin of the spoken stone
your scattered tresses serve your slender center
and the set sun and the sunken boat
not knowing any longer than you the unparted.

Telle tu brilles ondules ma dorée d'osiers
je tiens ta main de dalle et de palais mouillé
        où tout vient et se plaint
        tu n'as pas fait de nid
        sans dédain ni chagrin
forêt de mes épées sous signe entier tu dors
        sous arbre total j'aime.

As you ripple shine my golden one of withies
I hold your hand of stone slab and moistened palate
        where all come and complain
        you've not made a nest
        without disdain or grief
forest of my swords under whole sign you sleep
        under the entire tree I love.

ELLES PARLENT LES mères avec de telles voix d'argent
portées dans les épis pour ne pas toucher terre
retrouver le parfum dans la maison rentrée
aux murs des odeurs d'araignée et de poupée
des enfants tout en bas des yeux y peuvent jouer

Sur un lit de bois sur un lit de camp
voici mai mon amour

Aux balcons de paille et de soleil sont les femmes des choses
les hommes montent au ciel sans laisser leurs os
de l'un à l'autre sans relâche les oiseaux
quand la terre donne l'exemple
je sais de cercles de chaux ornée et de pétales de pâques

Toi qui tournes
folle à genoux d'où vient l'aurore
avec ta bouche de planète du soir d'herbe couchée
à la colline à la rosée tu es restée
cependant qu'en rêve il devenait de plus en plus impossible
[de fleurir.

Le bol tibétain qui court la montagne
le bois dur le jour sans voyelles blanches
plonger dans le puits des troupeaux fermés
où des rois droits rouges et noirs abattent
éternels des lettres vives sur des tables.

Dormons sur le bois et les monts drapés
du côté sans fleurs où ne sont plus là
les rideaux de lune où bouge l'aimée

Les fleurs crient dans la bouche
si douces pour se venger
les trèfles la pluie

THE MOTHERS THEY speak with such silver voices
carried through the corn so as not to touch the earth
collecting the perfume in the homecoming house
fragrances of spider and doll on the walls
the children down below the eyes can play there

On a bed of wood on a wooden cot
this is May my love.

On balconies of straw and sun are the women of things
the men climb to the sky without leaving their bones
the birds restlessly relay between the one and the other
when the earth gives the example
I know of circles of ornate quicklime and easter petals

You who spin
kneeling madwoman from whom the aurora descends
with your mouth of twilight planet of grass stretched out
in the hill in the dew you remained
however while dreaming it became ever more impossible
to bloom.

The Tibetan bowl which roams the mountain
the hard wood the day without white vowels
plunging into the well of closed herds
where kings dismantle red and black laws
eternal letters illuminated on the tables.

Let us sleep on the wood and curtained mountains
on the side without flowers where no longer are
the curtains of moon where the beloved moves

Flowers cry within the mouth
so sweet as to avenge
the clovers the rain

naine compagnie
leurs mille petits bras aux fenêtres du grenier

Adieu dans mon beau carrosse
le décor s'en va des chênes
la reine gît contente sur la table
froids de très loin sont perdus les feuillages
chez elle sous ses yeux la folle sans ramages

Sur un lit de bois sur un lit de camp
voici mai mon amour.

a miniature company
their thousand little arms in the windows of the attic

Farewell in my fine carriage
the scenery takes leave of the oaks
the queen lies content on the table
cold from afar lost are the leaves
at home beneath her eyes the madwoman without design

On a bed of wood on a wooden cot
this is May my love.

Ô MA TOURTERELLE
allée se poser
dans les cavernes d'andrinoples rouges et d'osiers
la gorge chante

La coupe le croissant les dauphins du ciel blanc
aimer il faisait beau aimer il faisait jour
sous le ciel morte amour changé de talisman
belle engloutie de bleu joyeux et disparu
tes santals ont séché dans leurs voyelles d'eau.

Comment sous le ciel bas d'orages et d'ascètes
apparaissent encor ces fougères de mai
ta chambre de corail ma douce mousseline
où le soleil fermé sur le placard bougeait
et ta joue qui jamais ne connut le voyage
pétale de là-bas qui penchait comme un pré.

O MY ANGEL dove
gone to settle
in the caverns of rubia and wicker
the throat sings.

The chalice the crescent the dauphins of the white sky
love it was beautiful love it was day
beneath the sky dead lover altered talismans
a beauty swallowed by a joyous and vanishing blue
your sandalwoods have dried up in their vowels of water.

How under the sky low with storms and ascetics
these ferns of May come forth once more
your room of coral my sweet muslin
where the closed sun moves above the cupboard
and your cheek which never saw a voyage
a petal from elsewhere that spreads out like a meadow.

Les Magies
(1972)

Sorceries

Déméter

S'il est une pierre de tristesse j'y suis assise
Là où les bandelettes tombent obliques sur la plaine
Blancs voiles. Ceci est léger.
Où la déesse aux gros yeux trempe l'enfant des autres dans
[le feu.

L'arbre refuse de s'orienter. L'émeraude
Tient son poing fermé. S'il est
Une pierre de tristesse j'y suis assise.

Demeter

If it is a stone of sorrow there I am seated
There where ribbons fall oblique upon the plain
White veils. This weightlessness.
Where the wild-eyed goddess plunges the others' child in
the fire.

The tree refuses to orient itself. The emerald
Keeps its fist clenched. If it is
A stone of sorrow I am seated there.

Peau d'âne

C'était Peau d'âne dans la sphère
La belle chargée de voyance
La sphère de bijoux.

Travaille chagrin travaille
La lanterne filait le ferment faiblissait le gâteau bleuissait.

Il était vrai : tu me donnas dans la joie
Une robe couleur de temps
De quel jour de quel temps zéphir ô pluie ô nuit.

Peau d'âne

There was Peau d'âne in the realm
The beauty who knew all
The realm of prized rubies and gems.

Work grief work
The lantern spinning, the leaven weakening, the wedding cake
going blue

It was true: happily you gave me
A dress the color of time
From which day what weather zephyr o rainfall o night.

Le Berger

Berger affolé de fées
Toute science oubliée
À vau-l'eau le vent la lune.

Danse en peau de hyènes
Aux chambres des planches
Et pour la sarabande
Douce amère l'Antique
Tant soit peu souriante
Te fera vis-à-vis
En beaux sabots dorés.

Puis vous vous nourrirez d'argent salé
Avec l'eau qui court dessus dessus.

Et quand ce sera assez
Des colloques désordonnés
Des cadeaux et des raisons

Tu laisseras les bougies et les ombres au plafond
Tu laisseras l'éternelle dépitée en ses cheveux
Chargée brillante près du feu récriminant aux poutrelles

Et tu partiras là-haut
Où la sibylle tourne
Les améthystes et le vent.

The Shepherd

Shepherd stricken by the fae
Every science forgotten
Down the drain the wind the moon.

Dancing in hyena skin
In wood plank rooms
And for the saraband
Bittersweet Ancient
Slightly smiling
Will meet you
In beautiful golden hooves.

Then you will feed yourself salted silver
With water which runs on top atop.

And when that is enough
Of the chaotic gatherings
Of the gifts and reasons

You will leave the candles and shadows on the ceiling
You will leave the eternal one vexed in its tendrils
Charged bright by the fire protesting against the beams

And you will go up there
Where the sibyl spins
Amethysts and wind.

La Saint-Jean

Après l'ondine marche et vient la salamandre
La rousse du Jourdain en feu
— Saint-Jean des templiers et de l'airain des salamandres —

Comment la fée porte son deuil
Petit ange violet
Ceci me fut révélé
Sur le chemin à midi
                                        Dieu le sait.

Les fées ont le cœur gros toujours et bondissant
Le lièvre le sait et le fait
                                        C'est la Saint-Jean.

Source source source
Chemin de ton bruit
Source toujours source
                                        C'est la Saint-Jean.

Day of St. John

After the undine walks and the salamander comes
The redhead of Jordan ablaze
—Saint John of the templars, salamander bronze—

How the faerie bears her loss
Tiny violet angel
This was revealed to me
High noon on the path
                    God knows it.

The fae are forever heavy-hearted and bounding
The hare knows it and does it
                    This is St. John.

Source source source
Path of your sound
Source always source
                    This is St. John.

Les Troupeaux

Les enfants animaux passaient les monts vers des buts
Sous Orion sous Jupiter entiers
Les étoiles regardaient clouées
Avancer les sabots ternes.

À la vitre je pleurais des étoiles.
Les sabots se mouvaient de plus en plus là-haut
Des gouttes de lait sur la rosée
Tombaient secrètement des femelles en marche.

En toi ô nuit manteau de laine noire des bergers.

The Flocks

Animal children passed goalward through the mountains
Under Orion under Jupiter entire
The stars watched confined
Advancing their ashen hooves.

Against the window I wept stars
The hooves moving further and further above
Drops of milk on the dew
Fell secretly from marching ewes.

All within you o night black fleece of shepherds.

Vénus

Que font les amants ils s'aiment et se tourmentent
Aiment et se tourmentent pour pouvoir s'aimer encore
[un peu plus loin
Et d'être tant passés et repassés sous leurs propres arbres
Ils gisent clairsemés les bras défaits dans la forêt
Mâchant encor des bouts de flèches et de branches.

Inoccupés constants commençant et laissant
Troupeau charmant gardé au bois de la magie
Par la plus forte et plus nonchalante des mains

Que font amants ils s'aiment et se tourmentent.

Leurs parlers leur langage
Leurs perles leurs abeilles
Leur force coutumière
Quand des déesses d'aube
La fière chasse à courre

Puis l'antique quiétude.

Que font amants ils s'aiment et se tourmentent.

Venus

What do lovers do they love and torment
Love and torment in order to love a little further still
And to be passed and passed again under their own trees
They lie scattered arms unraveled in the forest
Gnawing tips of fleche and branch.

Unoccupied unchanging starting stopping
Charming herd kept in the spellbound wood
By the strongest and most nonchalant of hands

What do lovers do they love and torment.

Their idioms their language
Their pearls their bees
Their customary strength
When goddesses of dawn
Proudly sound the hunt

Then the ancient stillness.

What do lovers do they love and torment.

Verseau

Mon frère nettoie ton fusil
À la porte du seigneur.
Les tristes échassiers sont vendus par le ciel
Depuis ce Janvier dans la ville du capitaine
Où se tordaient — à l'ouest la seule primevère —
Les cheveux suffoqués de notre mère jeune.

Aquarius

My brother cleans your rifle
At the baron's door.
The pitiful bitterns are sold by the sky
Since this January in the captain's village
Where writhing—to the west the lone primrose—
The suffocated hair of our young mother.

Capricorne

Il y a dans l'air une odeur de noir animal
Il y a dans l'air glacé une odeur militaire
Un claquement verni tel d'un bec de vautour
                                        Sous le ciel obéi.

Je suis sur un banc comme l'épervier se perche
Un uniforme ancien se ternit dans les branches.
Et je pense à des capitaines
Dont la femme croyante et suffocante enfante
Face à la fenêtre
Par la nuit de Janvier.

Capricorn

There is in the air a black animal odor
There is in the air a frigid military odor
A lacquered snap like a vulture's beak
                                        Under the despotic sky.

I am on a bench as the sparrowhawk perches
An old uniform fading in the branches.
And I think about captains
Whose wife supplicating and suffocating gives birth
In front of the window
By January night.

La Châtelaine d'Oueil

La châtelaine d'Oueil a perdu la mémoire
Dans le grand vent du nord elle a perdu le boire
Elle a fait de sa chambre une haute montagne.

Les troupeaux et la pluie ont descendu les pentes
Avec tous les poignards des cloches de septembre
Ils sont entrés au seuil de cette cathédrale
Cœur mince et si offert des châtelaines d'Oueil.

Et haussant dans ses mains la creuse solitude
L'incalculable hiver et à venir le rien
Heureuse de l'écho glacé de l'eau intacte
La châtelaine d'Oueil a perdu la mémoire.

Chatelaine of the Vallée d'Oueil

The chatelaine of Oueil has lost her memory
In the great northern wind she lost her drink
And fashioned a tall mountain out of her bedroom.

Flocks and rain run down the hills
With all the dirks of September bells
They crossed the threshold of that cathedral
The paltry heart so offered by the chatelaines of Oueil.

And raising in her hands the hollow solitude
The incalculable winter and the nothingness ahead
Pleased with the icy echo of unbroken water
The chatelaine of Oueil has lost her memory.

Gilles des Rais

Eau secoue la pluie des toits
Celle des châteaux du lierre
C'était vert l'eau bouillonnait.

Ce furent des draperies
Tiges antique garnison
Chœurs cachés des Mélusines
Sous de feutrées floraisons.
Jamais étoile du berger
Ne montra du si féerique
Il n'était plus soir ni jour.

Au long battant à la longue aile
Terrifiant
Toi l'aîné le seul le lierre.

Il y eut un tel sourire
Quand ce fut le nid de feu
Parmi le cierge et la fleur
Un plat sourire de pierre
Une Lilith toute blanche
Grande géante là-haut
Au-dessus du nid de feu.

On ne pouvait arriver
À plus vieille sécurité
À plus sereine bienveillance
Dans les bras d'avant Adam
Au cercle des démons blancs.

Disons disons
Le cœur marron

Gilles de Rais

Water shakes the rain from the roofs
Those of ivy castles
T'was green the boiling water.

There were tapestries
Embellishing ancient stems
Choruses concealed from the Melusines
Underneath the dampened deluges.
Never did the evening star
Appear so otherworldly
No longer night nor day.

By the long beat of the long wing
Horrifying
You the firstborn the only the ivy.

There was one such smile
When this was the nest of fire
Among the votive and the flower
A placid smile of stone
A Lilith all in white
Great giantess up there
Up above the nest of fire.

We couldn't attain
An older safety
A calmer benevolence
In the arms before Adam
In a circle of white demons.

Say, let's say
The chestnut heart

Noir de baies boules chatons
Résidus violets des haies
Fruit de fusain
Oui zinzolin
Et laurier-tin

Manche étain talisman plomb
Car il est une saison
Où l'on relève la garde.

Là
La belette saut comme une guerrière le château hurle
Y suivent des manches de couleurs sans noms
On revient
— Peut-être encore un matin perlé une rose blanche —
Puis traînant ces ailes et ces manches somptueuses
[il faut tuer.

Black of berries balls kittens
Violet residues of hedgerows
Spindle fruit
Yes zinzolin
And laurestine

Tin sleeve lead talisman
For it is the season
To relieve the guard.

There
The weasel leaps like a warrior the castle wails
There follows sleeves of nameless colors
We return
—Perhaps once more a pearly morning a white rose—
Then dragging those wings and those extravagant sleeves you must kill.

Château de Forchtenstein

Les dames de Hongrie ne mangent plus
Mélangées aux dames d'Autriche
Dans le fort château suspendues.
Leur plus bel amant
Sur le plancher beige
Debout il ne bouge
Plus dans son costume.

Les couleurs orange
Les occupations
Comitats gardés
Bornes constellées
Le long des halliers
De majuscules de couronnes et de portes.

Je passe les portes le voûtes les bornes
Pour aller cueillir par voies magnifiques
Pour aller chercher les irréprochables
Racines et toutes plantes valables
Dans le temps du cerf celui des duvets.

Le roi sous le dais. Il a des guirlandes
Très blanches de bras comme des muguets
Le roi sous le dais. Il a des bougies
Des grands yeux luisants les faciles coupes

Quand le vent du nord vous voit sous la porte.

Chateau de Forchtenstein

The ladies of Hungary no longer dine
Combined with the ladies of Austria
Suspended in the castle fort.
Their most beautiful lover
On the beige floor
Standing he moves not
No more in costume.

The colors orange
The pastimes
Guarded warbands
Constellated curbstones
All along the thickets
Capital letters crowns and doors.

I pass the doors the vaults the curbstones
To go harvest by magnificent paths
To go searching for the irreproachable
Roots and all acceptable plants
In the age of the stag that of thistledown

King under the canopy. His garlands milk white
And arms like lilies of the valley
The King under the canopy. His candles
Huge glistening eyes the pleasing cups

Then the north wind sees you from under the door.

Le Templier

Dans la forêt nantie de vent et de nards celtiques
De ce que l'on n'avait jamais plus ouï dire
Menée par les graines des plantes tombées du coin
Du tablier des nièces des Templiers

Livrée suivons qui fait fleurir et germer
Qui reste et qui écrase.

Tiz tiz. Au caché les mésanges
Des syriennes complaisances
Le Templier au monument
De la forêt de vent et de nard celtique.

L'esprit dans le bois descend.

The Templar

In the forest rich with wind and celtic nard
With what was never heard uttered again
Guided by the seeds of plants fallen from the corner
Of the Templar nieces' smocks

In livery follow what brings flowering and sprouts
What lingers and erases.

Tizh Tizh. In hiding the chickadees
From Syrian indulgences
The Templar at the monument
Of the forest of wind and celtic nard.

Spirit descends into wood.

Les Templiers de Pierrefitte

Sous les grands reflets de fonte violette
Avec le lierre l'emblème de toison
Qu'ils dorment à l'arc brisé. Poignée d'épée
Croix luxure rentrées ordre des saisons.

Là-haut en haut de ce blé parcimonieux
Plus d'engrangements. La stérile violette.
Plus de frère à deux ni d'automnes équestres
Plus de norme d'Orient. Dormez Templiers.

The Templars of Pierrefitte

Under the great reflections of the violet thaw
With the ivy the insignia of fleece
At the broken arch they sleep. Sword in hand
Carnal cross order of the seasons returned.

Up there above this parsimonious wheat
No more harvests. Violet wasteland.
No more paired brothers nor cavalier autumns
No more Eastern custom. Sleep, Templars. Sleep.

Chœurs des Reines du Pays de Kousch

Là où sont les étoiles
Tournait une perdrix
Elle tournait la terre
De la Mère Kàli.

Le sexe de fleur bleue
Qui grimpe à la liane
Ici c'est la violette.
— Que je sois que tu sois heureuse —

Pour plaire à sa compagne
A boité la femelle
Dans la danse du cycle
Quand Vénus descendait.

Peu sévères sont les rives d'Ionie
La mer Noire voilà se borde de chevaux
Le nuage s'abaisse et l'étoilée perdrix
Sous l'acanthe expirée ne saura plus danser.

L'étoile fait sa nuit la lune tient son feu.
Nous hases des îles mitrées
Biens de Vénus de noire Asie
Encore un peu chantons nous l'avons cru
Sous les chapiteaux marins confondues :

« D'où te viennent ces beaux yeux cernés perdrix
[de plumes ? »
— Que je sois que tu sois heureuse —

Choirs of Queens from the Kingdom of Kush

There where the stars are
Turns a partridge
She turned the earth
Of the Mother Kali.

Sex of blue flower
Which climbs to the liana
Here it is the violet
—That I may be that you may be happy—

To please her companion
The female limped
Into the dance of the cycle
As Venus descended.

Hardly harsh are the edges of Ionia
Here the Black Sea is lined with horses
The clouds drape down and the starry partridge
Under the expired acanthus can no longer dance.

The stars make her night the moon keeps her fire.
We wild jills of mitered islands
The goods of Venus of blackest Asia
We sing a little more having thought
Under the confused marine columns:

"Whence come these beautiful ringed eyes feathered partridge?"
—That I may be that you may be happy—

L'Agapanthe

La triste agapanthe de Vienne
Bleue comme ce palais du dimanche vu par elle
Je me délivre de l'air même
Des gentils siècles en arrière

Si facile il m'est si facile
À travers les murs d'interroger le cœur des abdiqués
Sans pleureuses sans bruits. Ce n'est plus dans la rue
C'est vers cette cour beige que tout se retourne.
Un seul érable humide et sous les longues pierres
Courant comme souris la dernière nichée de merles
Avec la ruse dans les yeux.

L'empereur dort

Par là au-dedans.

Abolis les tourments. C'est le bastion la plaine
La force des chevaux des bêtes qu'on amène
Par le licol griffons des basilics des onces
Des dragons en troupeaux à la nuit menés paître.

Incalculable vie. Assise sur la pierre
Où les merles rampaient le dimanche passait
Et j'entendais tinter l'émeraude et l'épée
Les magiques fourreaux nus sur des cramoisis.

Pour prédire il faut se conserver
Un cœur d'une main
Une agapanthe en boule de l'autre
Ce sont les signes du royaume.

Agapanthus

The sad agapanthus of Vienna
Blue like this Sunday palace seen by her
I am delivered from the air itself
Of gentle centuries past

So easy it is so easy for me
To interrogate through walls the heart of the abdicated
Without the wailing without sounds. It is no longer in the road
It is toward this beige court that everything returns.
A single maple and dewy under the long stones
Running like mice the last brood of blackbirds
With ruse in its eyes.

The emperor sleeps

Inside, just through there.

Abolish turmoil. It is the bastion the plane
The strength of horses and beasts that we lead
Griffons by the harness basilisks snow leopards
Flocks of dragons led to graze in the night.

Incalculable life. Seated there on the stone
Where creeping blackbirds would spend Sunday
And I hear the tinkling of emerald and the sword
The magical sheaths naked upon crimsons.

In order to predict one must preserve
A heart in one hand
A ball of agapanthus in the other
For these are the signs of the kingdom.

Je te laisse agapanthe fleur douce inexistante
Ô brume belle de fleur bleue
Tournée vers ce point cardinal du dimanche
Qui n'exista jamais que toujours je connais.

I leave you agapanthus sweet imaginary flower
O beautiful brume of blue flower
Turned towards this cardinal point of Sunday
Which never existed but I have always known.

Au Lierre

Je quitte chevaliers et purs hennins et neige
La tour
Et de la maison de merle
Toi le blason toi le lierre.

Veuve des astres du septentrion quand je partirai quand
[je m'en irai quand loin j'irai

J'emporterai
Un bouquet de graines de lierre
Joyaux du vert éternel.

Et du jasmin blanc du stéphanotis
De tout ce qui est blanc de tout ce qui est lis
Je n'aurai jamais ce baptême amer
De ta dure feuille en la nuit d'hiver
Trempée raclant à l'obscure vitre
Triste oiseau triste cœur.

In Ivy

I leave the knights and pure hennins and snow
The tower
The house of the blackbird
You the crest you the ivy.

Hyperborean astral widow when I depart when I leave when far
I will go

I will carry with me
A bundle of ivy seeds
Jewels of eternal green.

And with white jasmine with stephanotis
With all that is white and all that is lily
I will never suffer that bitter baptism
Of your hard leaf in the winter night
Drenched scraping at the dark window
Sad bird sad heart.

La Verte

Mousse herbe et toi graminée fleur sa feuille
Monde de masse verte où s'avance la dame
Si hautement coiffée et de robes variées
Distraite et tournant partout son col d'oiseau.

Et le chêne veillait épais sur ta venue
Connaissant de tout temps vieux serviteur parfait
Ta robe de septembre et ta robe de mai.

The Green Woman

Moss herb and you grass flower its leaf
World of green matter where the lady advances
Hair piled high as heaven and varied of gown
Amused, her bird neck turns all around.

The thick oak loomed over your arrival
Knower of all time perfect ancient servant
Your gown of September and your gown of May.

Chanson

Notre chambre suspendue
Au creux du ciel
Hors des lames de la pluie
Hors des larmes de la lune.

Au bas des murs sont les tournois
Et les orties nous ne les verrons pas.

La lune a parlé de nuit je ne sais pas
La nuit l'emmène courir
Sur la rive et dans son lit
De nuit.

Ceci cela jusqu'à l'aube du jour
Qui fait rentrer les salamandres.

Song

Our room suspended
In the hollow of the sky
Beyond the rain's spears
Beyond the moon's tears.

Beneath walls are the tourneys
And stinging nettles they will go unnoticed.

The moon spoke of a night unknown to me
The night takes her running
Along the bank and in its bed
Of darkness.

This that until the break of day
Calls the salamanders home.

Nuit

La nuit d'hiver reviendra-t-elle
Pour me reposer prés de toi.
Les façades boiront sévères
Le clair de lune et sa lumière
Sera chassée de nos baisers et de nos bras.

La chambre est là seule et rideaux fermés
Tu es là seule avec tes yeux fermés
Le clair de lune est le clair de tes bras
Et la nuit porte l'insouciant navire.

Night

The winter's night will it return
For me to rest near you.
The façades will gravely drink
Moonlight and its wisdom
Will be driven from our kisses and arms.

The room is there alone curtains closed
You are there alone with your closed eyes
The moonlight being the light of your arms
And night carries this tranquil ship.

Poème

Accueille-moi dans ton berceau
Il est brûlant et de tout temps
C'est la boîte des diligences
C'est lui qui longe la forêt
De tous les voleurs d'Allemagne.

Des saintes portées du lièvre
Il est l'éternel habitat
La jeune sorcière innocente
Les tend le long du voyage
Nous les tend à bout de bras.
Les rideaux de cuir l'orage.

Un oiseau aux grandes ailes
A fait un nid désolé
D'innombrables pèlerinages y sont allés
— Hurlez vous plus que pleurez
Mes solennels défilés —

Avec un couteau de roses
Dans l'acier de ses jointures
Dans son passé de métal
L'oiseau frappé ne maudit pas
Il meurt davantage
— Meurs petite mouche noire —

Dans un vase d'écailles
D'écailles et de lin
Roide et noir je vais bien
Bien demander à boire.

Poem

Welcome me into your cradle
It is aflame and for all time
It is the stagecoach box
It is what runs along the forest
Of all the thieves of Germany.

It is the eternal habitat
Of sacred litters of hare
The innocent young sorceress
Stretches them along the voyage
We hold them at arm's length.
Leather curtains the storm.

A bird with great wings
Has built a desolate nest
Where innumerable pilgrimages have gone
—Scream more than cry
You solemn procession—

With a knife of roses
In the steel of its joints
In its history of metal
A stricken bird curses not
It dies a little more
—Die little black fly—

In a vase of scales
Scales and flax
Steep and black I am fine
To ask for a drink.

C'est le monastère droit
Sur le promontoire étroit

Un seul lis dans la vallée.
C'est à prendre ou à laisser
Pour l'occasion d'un seul lis
Il fait mille fois plus nuit.

Faillait-il qu'une brillante
Me rappelât tout le bien
— Mouche il faut bien que tu meures —
Nous nous périrons au-delà
À la façon des rosées
Sur le trésor de la nuit.

Il faut que je m'en aille
À cause de la pluie
Suivie de capricornes
Qui m'obéissent bien.

Long poème comme un long fleuve
Va à qui aimera.

It is the monastery upright
On the narrow path

A lone lily in the valley.
Take it or leave it
For the possibility of a single lily
It is night a thousand times more.

Must it take a brilliance
To remind me of all the good
—Fly you surely must die—
We will perish ourselves on the other side
In the manner of dewdrops
On the treasures of night.

I must go away
Because of the rain
Followed by capricorns
Who obey me well.

Long poem like a long river
Flows to whoever will love.

La Source

La source est là dans le plancher
Mange autour la fête brillante
Les astres luisants ont ciré
D'anciens insectes allumé.

Comme en un gazon où s'étonnent
À plat et d'or scellées les fleurs
Alentour le petit orchestre
Les chaises de jardin. La chouette pleure.
Qui ne pleure pas.

Montant l'escalier feutré
Vers l'eau froide à la Chandeleur
J'attends je m'attends
Sans nourriture je sais où manger ailleurs.
Voilà le ton de la demeure
Non pas pauvre non pas obscure
Non plus vivante mais si sûre.

L'orchestre est parti. Les étoiles rangées.
Les chaises ordonnées. Ô plancher de chêne
Tantôt c'est la neige
Et tantôt les cires
Et toi rêvée pure
La nonne lunaire
Viens boire à la source
La source de bois.

Ouvrez venez à la fontaine
Ce qui n'avait jamais brillé va venir.

The Spring

The spring is there in the floor
Eating around the luminous festivity
The glimmering cosmos polished
With ancient burning insects.

Like in a lawn where they are surprised
Laid flat and gold sealed flowers
Surrounding the tiny orchestra
The garden chairs. The owl weeps.
Who weeps not.

Climbing the felted staircase
Toward the cold water of Candlemas
I wait I wait in suspense
Without nourishment. I know where else to feed.
Here is the tone of the dwelling
Not weak not obscure
No longer vital but so certain.

The orchestra is gone. The stars put back in place.
Chairs arranged. O oak floor
Sometimes it's snow
And sometimes wax
And you pure dream
Lunar nun
Coming to drink at the spring
The spring of wood.

Open. Come to the fountain
What has never shone will come.

La Folle des Sargasses

à Jean Rhys

Ne retourne pas obscure
Vers l'oranger amer.

À la cime les arbres
Les pirates entiers
Remuent dans les îles
De tes yeux tes cheveux.

Nous irons aux Antilles
Ise folle
Voir le stéphanotis sur la rampe de fer.

La goyave la mangue
S'incrustent à la maison
Moisie. Luciole et blatte
Trouent de leur poison
Ton corps long dans la chambre.

La basque et la violette
Luxe entêté te mènent
À la perte certaine
Du voyage. Adieu.
Bientôt bientôt.

Le cheval part l'oiseau se fixe
Entre les sourcils obstinés
Où sont les pirates. L'oiseau
De montagne. Sa note unique et solitaire.

Madwoman of Sargassum

for Jean Rhys

Don't look back forlorn
Toward the bitter orange tree.

At the peak the trees
The unscathed pirates
They stir in the isles
Of your eyes your hair.

We will go to the Antilles
Wild Isis
To see the stephanotis on the iron rail.

Guava mango
Incrusted into the decaying
House. Firefly and cockroach
Their poison penetrates
Your long body in the bedroom.

Skirt and veil
Stubborn luxury leads you
To the definite loss
Of the journey. Farewell.
So long. Soon soon.

The horse leaves the bird fixed
Between the obstinate brows
Where the pirates are. The mountain
Bird. Its unique and solitary note.

Jaune le carton
Des corridors longs
Et comme une terreur effondrée
La robe rouge qui sentait la poussière et la pluie.

Ne retourne pas obscure
Vers l'oranger amer.

Yellow the cardboard
Of long corridors
And like a collapsed terror
The red dress which smelled like dust and rain.

Don't look back forlorn
Toward the bitter orange tree.

Tantum Ergo

Dormons sur les oreilles
Des Tantum Ergo roux.

Le chat du matin rentre sous la planète
Elle pend seule dans ses piques de cristal.
Mais tout étant brassé la famille l'été
Une autre aube et prairie
Sur l'autel embaumé
Plan de satin de joie
S'installe à mi-soirée
S'habille le Tantum Ergo.

Dans le drap couleur ciel des choses arrangées
Sautent et brillent en musique
Les anneaux boucles d'oreilles
De la Juive immaculée.

Débordant l'ouïe fine
Des milliers de saphirs
Coquent et s'entrechoquent
Puis va le chant bien endigué et grand
Roulant l'antique document des jubilants.

Qui sait quoi. À la voûte des pigeons couvent et traversent
Au bec de corinthiennes écailles d'or
Et Vénus se relève
Plus que blanche et que bleue.

Sur les grandes oreilles
Des Tantum Ergo roux
Dormons plus démunis
Qu'un chat dans la caverne
Que vous dire ô cierges

Tantum Ergo

We sleep on the ears
Of the red Tantum Ergo.

The cat of day slinks back under the planet
She dangles alone among her crystal pikes.
But all being confused the family the summer
Another dawn and meadow
Upon the perfumed altar
Map of satin and joy
Settles in mid evening
Dresses the Tantum Ergo.

Things arranged in the sky-blue sheet
Leaping and twinkling in music
The ring hooped earrings
Of the immaculate Jew.

Exalting keen ears
Thousands of sapphires
Colliding and jostling
Thus goes the song restrained and great
Rolling up the age-old document of jubilation.

Who knows what. In the vault pigeons brood and cross
At the beak of Corinthian golden scales
And Venus rises once more
Beyond the white and the blue.

On the great ears
Of the red Tantum Ergo
We sleep more defenseless
Than a cat in a cave
O candles, what can I say.

Tenerife I

El Carrito

Et le carrito Messieurs
De la Grande Ourse étoilée ?
Féerie du bois sacré
Les enfants rient de l'été.

Seuls aux bancs des économes entr'eux et des prophètes
Quelques-uns parlant bien dans l'espace des branches.

Ce paradis tire des cruches et des herbes
Ce paradis mange de nuit
Quand les grillons sont aux racines
L'oiseau au nid l'abeille prés.

Tu vas enfant boudeur des sommeils des jardins
Tard dans la nuit où tes pères nourriciers se croisent
Des mâles aquatiques détiennent la place
Des Jupiters muets sont installés aux astres.

Mais la pluie lisse le vent
Et demain chacun son tour
La Grand Ourse et ses rubans
Auront raison des époux.

Tenerife I

El Carrito

And the carrito gentlemen
From the bestarred Ursa Major?
Fairyland the sacred wood
The children laugh with summer.

Alone on the bookkeepers' benches between them and the
        prophets
People speaking deep into the space of the branches.

This paradise pulls pitchers and herbs
This paradise eats night
When the crickets are in the roots
The bird in its nest the honeybee near.

Go, child, sullen with the sleepiness of gardens
Late in the night where your nourishing fathers cross paths
Aquatic males holding place
Mute Jupiters arranged in the heavens.

But the rain smoothens the wind
And tomorrow each in turn
The Ursa Major and its ribbons
Will be proven right about the grooms.

Tenerife II

El Verdino (Le chien vert)

De la hauteur de la chambre
Laide comme un fort dans cette ville de loisir et de plaisir
De ces mains vertes qui entrent d'arbres
Je dis
Que je voudrais un chien vert.

Madame qu'as-tu fait aux gens
Pour qu'ils t'aiment et ne t'aiment pas
Pour rire et pour pleurer tant eux et toi ?

Ayant vue sur de grands insensibles lauriers
Faits pour les avenues sans gloire et abriter
Allumée à mon propre feu comme une médaille
J'ai ramassé l'éclat de l'île et à mon poing
À mes blasons à mes côtés
Je vous le dis
Je voudrais un chien vert.

Car je suis tournée à l'est
À mon est est la goyave
Et quand le soir reviendra
Aura très peur la médaille.
Ce parc peu sûr est contre vous dans ses habits
Les araignées dessous y marchent en armées
Sous la fiancée inerte au banc de son soldat.
Des lilas peu gentils y dévorent la nuit
De fiels verts exhalés qui vous feront souffrir
Aussi sur le banc noir des fiancées et soldats.

Il y a des cristaux inouïs transparents
Pour les noces des gens qui ne savent pas quoi

Tenerife II

El Verdino (The Green Dog)

From the height of this bedroom
Ugly as a fortress in this town of leisure and pleasure
Of those green hands reaching into the trees
I say
I would like a green dog.

Madame what have you done to the people
For them to love and not love you
Laughing so and crying so them and you?

Having gazed over the unfeeling laurels
Made for gloriless avenues and for shelter
Lit by my own fire like a medallion
I collected the luster of the isle and in my palm
In my shield at my sides
I tell you:
I would like a green dog.

For I turned to the east
To my east there is guava
And when the evening returns
It will fear the medallion.
This precarious park is against you in its ways
Spiders march below it in legions
Beneath the betrothed inert on the bench of her soldier.
There lilacs scarcely kind devour the night
Of exhaled green biles which too will torment you
On the black bench of soldiers and their betrotheds.

There are crystals unheard of and clear
For the marriages of men who know not what

Et sont le perroquet et le chien de quinquet
Dans leur île étoilée en son trottoir sans garde.

Quelqu'un m'a dit passe à l'ombre
M'a dit passer dans le fiel
Et j'ai trouvé la colonne
Tournante à l'église morte.

Voilà pourquoi je veux cette chose tangible
Un chien vert de conquêtes chevronné de pistes
Où les sceaux sont frappés sur une peau de feuille
Et durement mené par l'île aux doigts de pierre.

« Je sais depuis longtemps
Ce qui me reste à faire
Et de tous mes verdinos
Et mes voix de cratère. »

Les femmes mages sont debout ont marché se sont assises
Avec leur petit chapeau leur mante sont allées prédire
Prédire à l'envers.
Les chiens ont mangé toutes les feuilles de Tacoronte
Puis ils ont hurlé
Dans les siècles
En amont de leurs mères
La chanson d'aujourd'hui

Et râlons tordons crions
Sans savoir pourquoi
Petits sans massues :

« Un rat a descendu
Reprisant une chaussette
Un autre rat a monté
Rapiéçant un caleçon
La grande rue del Castillo. »

Who are the parrot and the quinquet dog
On their bestarred island on their unattended block.

Someone told me to go through the shade
Told me to go into the bile
And I found the column
Spinning at the dead church.

This is why I want these intangible things
A green dog of conquests seasoned by the streets
Where the sigils are struck upon the leafy skin
And wrenched through the island with stone fingers.

"For long I have known
What remains to be done
And of all my verdinos
And my concave voices."

The wise women stood walked sat
Went with their little hood their mantle to divine
Foreseeing backwards and upside down.
The dogs ate all the leaves in Tacoronte
Then upstream from their mothers
They howled today's anthem
Into the centuries.

Let us rage writhe shriek
Without knowing why
So small without bludgeons:

"A rat went down
Mending a shoe
Another one went up
Darning their drawers
The great road of Castillo."

Uncollected Poems

Downshire Hill

13 juillet 1941

C'étaient les flaques d'eau du plein été, des chats —
de frais rideaux tordus tard le matin, la rue
partait comme une bohémienne avec ses cretonnes
de l'amour pas fini que le vent gonflait dehors.
Derrière les maisons ce n'est pas comme devant :
ça ment,
les maisons de Downshire Hill ;
on vit devant avec de la musique, sur une image,
on discute, on embrasse ses amis devant,
des couleurs y passent et de grands chevaux et
[des chariots
de lait — c'est rassurant, c'est au niveau du cœur.

Mais il y a les puits verts,
là où les ballons ont leurs racines,
où ils tombent et gémissent toutes nuits d'hiver.
Il y a des arbres si profonds,
des îles flottantes de salons ;
rien n'y mène tout y est coupé
et rêve intercepté ;
c'est les fous intercepté ;
c'est les fous verts —
La lune n'y est pas celle de la rue,
il s'en faut ; celle-là est des âmes perdues, des talus,
celle par où partent les morts de Londres,
par où s›avancent les avions tout menaçants.

Devant, la belle dame rit,
bat du pied contre la fenêtre,
change les choses, fait ce qu'il faut

Downshire Hill

July 31, 1941

Puddles of midsummer rain, cats—
New curtains twisted late in the morning, the road
took off like a bohemian with her scarves
of unresolved love billowed by wind.
        The front of the houses hide what's behind:
        they deceive,
        the houses of Downshire Hill;
        in front one lives with music, against an image,
        conversing, kissing friends,
        colors pass by there and great steeds and milk
        carts—it is reassuring, at the level of the heart.

                But there are green wells,
        where the balloons have their roots,
        where they fall and moan through winter nights.
        There are trees so deep
        floating islands of rooms;
        nothing arrives there, everything severed
        and every dream intercepted;
        madness intercepted;
        green madness—
That moon is not the one from the road,
        not remotely; she is for the lost souls, the embankments,
        the light by which the dead of London depart,
        by which the ominous planes advance.

        In front, the beautiful lady laughs,
        beats her foot against the window,
        changes things, does what she must
        with her fingers, with measure, with wonder.

avec les doigts, de la mesure, de l'émerveillement.
Elle parle dans les deux coins de sa bouche
avec le goût de la vie,
noire dans ses yeux parfois — mais la maison ne le
[sait pas.
Je sais tout.
La belle rue gonflée et jasminée
et dandinée comme celle
de Pondichéry à la mer,
quand le filao tord sous la pendule bleue
de l'église méthodiste sa forme habituelle
à des Coromandels sans soldats et sans pas.

Les chevaux du charbon, les chevaux du verglas
reviendront ; les ballons chanteront le grésil.

Il y a des fils
d'herbes partout ; le vent d'été chasse à midi
les herbes et les gens vers des comptoirs pour boire
aux amants, aux dards, aux soldats, aux gousses de
[Hampstead, aux fleurs
amies des bouteilles, le dimanche, comme chien et chat.

Éternellement les ballons s›enlèveront,
obéiront.
Le vert se venge.
Pendant tout le temps là où il est, nul ne connait,
grande flaque secrète à côté d'où l'on mange.
Il met de l'eau dans les vieux abris, et des souris,
et une salamandre laborieusement venue pour crever noyée.
Il se venge
avec des nénuphars, des tiges
autour des salons, des feuilles plus grandes que l'eau.

Le feu brûlait Londres,
devant, et du grenier c'était parfait

She speaks from both corners of her mouth
with a taste for life,
her eyes darken at times—but the house doesn't know.
I know everything.
The beautiful road billowed and jasmined
swaying like the one
from Pondicherry to the sea,
when the ironwood snakes under the blue pendulum
of the methodist church its usual formation
of coromandels without soldiers and without steps.

The charcoal horses, the black ice horses
will come back; the balloons will sing sleet.

There are the sons of grass
strewn everywhere; the summer wind hunts at noon
herbs and people toward the bars to drink
to the lovers, the spears, the soldiers, the Hampstead
violets, the flowers
bottle kissers, sunday, like dog and cat.

Eternally the balloons will rise,
will comply.
Green takes revenge.
For all this time, no one knew where it was,
a huge secret puddle next to where we eat.
It leaks water into old shelters, and mice,
and a salamander laboriously comes to drown to death.
It takes revenge
with water lilies, stems
throughout these rooms, leaves larger than the water.

The fire consumed London,
in front, and from the attic it looked perfect
it was a tremendous fear we knew;
two figures illuminated in their discussion

ça faisant une grande peur que l'on savait ;
deux figures illuminées en discutaient
on montait l'escalier et puis on descendait,
d'en bas, les wardens dans la rue amie vous réconfortaient
— il restait un gai pois de senteur par lui tout seul
à la grille, pas vu par le cheval du lait.

Mais la nuit de novembre, ah : ce qui s'est passé,
et celle de janvier — des troupeaux de Canaques
des marécages verts, faisaient contre-partie,
sans mot dire, tant qu'ils pouvaient,
dans ces jardins mauvais, au feu rouge, au feu gai
— on sait ce qu'il en est.

Ils sont restés,
pieds verts,
du côté
où ne sonne pas le bon troupeau avec ses pieds
imbus de devoir, et gais,
cachés du ballon qu'il faut plier
et des bombes incendiaires dans les terreaux.

Il faut des hérissons,
des fauves de Hampstead,
des yeux d'hiver
pour les canaques qui mangent après la salle à manger,
en rond, quand l'obus passe et le ciel est léger ;
et que la belle dame à la lumière mange
en leur tournant le dos.

Cette histoire empêchera
tous ceux qui ne sont pas fous
d'aller au jardin prier Vénus et cueillir les pois
for the Victory.

we went up the stairs then down,
from below, the wardens in the friendly road soothed you
—a ludic sweetpea remained all by itself
at the gate, unseen by the milk horse.

But November night, ah: what happened,
and that of January—the troop of Kanaks
from green marshes, were there in exchange,
without a word, as best they could,
in these evil gardens, in the red fire, in the ludic fire
—we know what it is.

They stayed,
feet green,
on the side
where the good troop's feet do not resound
imbued with duty, and ludic,
hidden from the balloon which must fold
and incendiary bombs in the fields.

We need hedgehogs,
Hampstead fauna,
winter eyes
for the Kanaks who eat behind the dining room,
in a circle, when mortar shell flies and the sky is weightless;
as the beautiful lady eats in the light
while turning her back to them.

This story will stop
all those who are not mad
from going into the garden to pray to Venus and pluck
        the peas
for the Victory.

Louange du Travail

à E.L.T. Mesens

J'avais compté sans falloir jeter les rames,
Reprendre le bec de la palombe noire,
Rendre à tour de bras des comptes.

À défaut de taureau tu n'as pas d'humour ;
Frotte à tour de bras si tu en as.
Seulement la lune, ainsi qu'à quelques autres, ne m'en avait
[pas fait.

Et tendrement bercée encore,
Bourgeonnant et d'autres tuant,
Quand ils bourgeonnaient on me tuait,
Petit porc de Pondichéry,
Petit porc de Chandernagor.

J'ai un ami qui vend des piques
A pour idole, un savon noir ;
Aussi il est propre tout noir
Il a de l'or fin plein de mousse
Il se répète mille fois en se tournant.

Avril avril je te dirai
Du haut du ciel tant de satins sont déchirés.
Je les écoute se fendre,
Tomber droits sur l'or des mousses.
La main à son oreille d'homme
La main qui les entend, on dit :
Venez, tout noirs, faire des paquets de satin.

Praise of Work

for E.L.T. Messens

I counted without needing to throw the oars,
Taking again the black wood pigeon's beak,
With all my might taking accountability.

With no taurus you have no humor;
Rub with all your strength if you have any.
Only the moon, just as it had a few others, inflicted nothing
upon me.

And tenderly rocked once more,
Some budding and others killing,
I was murdered when they blossomed,
Little pig of Pondicherry,
Little pig of Chandannagar.

I have a friend who sells pikes
Has for an idol a black soap;
Clean and entirely black
He has fine gold full of bubbles
Spinning he repeats himself a thousand times.

April April I will tell you
From the heights of the sky so many satins are torn.
I listen to them split,
Falling right over the sudsy gold,
The hand to its human ear
The hand which hears, it is said:
Come, completely black, to make satin bundles.

À mourir le vent d'avril
Des basses œuvres,
Et des bonnes œuvres,
Des œuvres de bourreau.

Tout est œuvre qui n'est pas moi le vent d'avril à mon oreille,
Tout n'est pas moi car je me nie le vent d'avril,
Je n'ai pas lancé de fabuleux signes couleur de violette,
Pas même pas même je ronge sous le cœur le travailleur
L'insecte arrête le laboureur
Et mon ami ne priera plus son savon noir.

La grande roue de la violette ses beaux doigts posés sur
[les têtes
Les tignasses d'Espagne et les autres
Évangiles noirs sueur au front, je vous arrête.
Vous avez tous bien travaillé. Félicités.

— Têtes, oiseaux serrés, femmes en cendres, violettes.

Londres, avril 1943

To die April wind
Of baser works,
And of good works,
The works of an executioner.

All work is not me April wind in my ear,
All is not me for I deny myself the April wind,
I did not cast fabulous signs the color of violets,
Not even not even, I eat away beneath the heart the worker
The insect stops the laborer
And my friend will no longer pray to his black soap.

The wide violet wheel its beautiful fingers poised on the heads
The manes of Spain and others
Black gospels with sweat on their brow, I arrest you.
You all have worked hard. Well done.

—Heads, taloned birds, women in ash, violets.

London, April 1943

Qui n'a pas tant d'amour disait le rossignol
ton bec n'a plus trempé dans toutes mes rosées
seul tu m'as délivré dans mes fils d'or pour rire
et tu laves du plomb au fond du seuil.

La lune
vient parfois habiter peut-être pas.

Joue
dans tes fils fatigant enfant gardé
de si loin qu'on oublie
le troupeau tellement léger et bouclé d'herbes

Lève les yeux pour rire
qui m'aime lève les yeux pour que je chante
à ces hauteurs sans ordre.

À l'ombre
du plomb je suis sous le seuil
ô l'ancienne bulle qui tinte.

Voici le rossignol, son doux théâtre
ses chevelures d'or charmé
ne se dressent ni main ni feuille.
Mais sous le seuil viennent ramper non adjurées
les mariées terribles du ver de la pierre

quand je lave du plomb
peut-être
en gardant la lune.

Avril 1946
(in *Cahiers d'Arts* 1945–1946)

WHO DOES NOT have this much love said the nightingale
your beak no longer buried in all my dews
you alone freed me to laugh within my golden threads
and you wash the lead deep in the threshold.

The moon
comes at times to dwell perhaps not.

Play
in your threads tiring minded child
from such a distance that we forget
the flock so ebullient with grassy locks.

Lift your eyes to laugh
whoever loves me lift your eyes so I may sing
at these disordered heights.

In the shadow
of lead I am under the threshold
o ancient chiming bubble.

Here is the nightingale, its gentle theater
its coiffure of charmed gold
raises neither hand nor leaf.
But under the threshold they come crawling unimplored
the terrible spouses of the worm of the stone

When I wash the lead
perhaps
while tending the moon.

April 1946
(in *Cahiers d'Arts* 1945–1946)

Gilles de Rais (II)

Un corbeau pour la droite le lierre pour la gauche
La vie durant.
La vie durant
Creuse est la tour.

Gilles de Rais et Dieu y promènent leurs manches
Des lambeaux reniés tant par l'autre que par l'un.
En quelque tourbillon de luttes et de lune
Ils vont s'assassinant interminablement
Pleurant front contre front sous la rusée horloge
Par là sous les feuillages
Arrêtée dans le vent.

Qu'allez qu'allez-vous faire
Rois de becs et de lierre ?
Faire souffrir le temps.

Gilles de Rais (II)

Crow for the right ivy for the left
Life enduring.
Life enduring
Hollow is the tower.

There Gilles de Rais and God walk their sleeves
Rags renounced as much by one as the other.
In some whirlwind of conflicts and moonlight
They proceed to murder without end
Crying face to face under the cunning clock
Through there under the leaves
Frozen in the wind.

What will what will you do,
King of beaks and ivy?
But force time to suffer.

À Paul

Tu disais nous ne sommes pas utiles
À porter les flambeaux de l'air nous sommes trop riches
Nous ne considérons pas le plomb nous ne mangeons pas
Entre la table et la fenêtre
Nous avons un accent d'étoiles
Et plus bonne volonté
À user nos mains que la taupe

Alors je te chanterai encore la chanson :

... Et la place d'Argos de plus en plus légère
Vous pleurerez où vous nommerez l'hirondelle
La gaze bleue et verte sous une autre main

La main couvre la mer.

Place forte d'honneur et val de l'éolienne
La main ne mange plus assiégée et rendue
Et la gorge s'arrête où est entré l'oiseau
De pépier à mourir au seuil des forteresses
L'air avait trop de creux d'extase pour conter
Et ces nids nourrissaient *le fidèle élusif*

... Et la place d'Argos de plus en plus légère
Et les nids pour chanter ce qui n'allait rien dire.

For Paul

You said we are useless
At carrying torches of air, we are too rich
We do not fret about the lead we do not eat
Between the table and the window
We have a celestial accent
And are more eager
To use our hands than a mole

And so I will sing this song to you once more:

...And the place of Argus grows slighter and slighter
You will cry where you name the swallow
Blue and green gauze beneath another hand

The hand covers the sea.

A place strong with honor and an aeolian valley
The hand no longer eats besieged and folded
And the throat stops where the bird came in
From chirping to dying on the threshold of fortresses
The air had too many rapturous hollows to count
And these nests fed *the elusive believer*

...And the place of Argus grows slighter and slighter
And the nests to sing what was to go unsaid.

Tombeau pour Marie-Berthe

Inconséquente gracieuse et morte
Toute la journée auprès des eaux croisées
Ou parallèles
Toi où étais-tu
Allée de ton pas ?

J'ai longé les eaux
J'ai longé la lune.

Nous sommes allées à la nacre à la perle de Février
Au petit château
Au château léger
Au château pesant de lourdes coupoles
Temples et tilleuls des siècles derniers
D'où tu étais sortie inconséquente gracieuse et morte.

Le gris des chatons celui des viviers tant de calmes eaux
Rien que fiers reflets façades posées.

L'eau claire faisait
Claire la rivière
Puis solennels l'argent et toi ternirent.

Toi où étais-tu
Par là de ton pas ?

Toute la journée
Et pour le moment
Longée accompagnée d'une lune diurne qui bleuissait
[le paysage

Tomb for Marie-Berthe

Reckless gracious and dead
All day beside waters
Intersecting or parallel
You where had you
Taken your step?

I walked along the waters
I walked along the moon.

We had gone to the nacre to February's pearl
To the little castle
The frivolous castle
To the castle weighed down with heavy belfries
Temples and lime trees from centuries past
Where you were released reckless gracious and dead.

The gray of pussy willows and fishponds, such calm waters
Nothing but proud reflections posed facades.

The water now clear
Clears the river
Then solemnly you and the silver tarnish.

You, where had you
Stepped over there?

All day
And for a moment
You ran along joined by a diurnal moon who bled blue over
  the landscape

J'ai longé les eaux
J'ai longé la lune.

L'idole le collier bleuissent
Déjà la bête au bois sauvage a crié
Le trésor cherche la clé.

Enfant voyageur Dieu te garde :
L'arc-en-ciel de toutes parts
Voici l'alliance et l'allegiance
Voici le pas.

I walked along the waters
I walked along the moon.

The muse her necklace turn blue
Already the beast has cried in the wildwood
Treasure seeks the key.

Wandering child, let God protect you:
Rainbows from all around
Here are the alliance and the allegiance
Here is the step.

La Taciturne

Attends couleur de Saturne
Qui joins et enseignes
En ton temps.
Au linteau marron parmi tes malles de pierre
Mangeant
Sous la mante
L'hiver la nourriture du prochain hiver
La même et même temps.

Incantatrice sourcilleuse
Reliant la feuille et la plume
Dans ton atelier des bois
Femme au trésor taciturne.

C'est ta seule joie quand tes doigts
Tiennent vers le couchant
De la grive la clavicule
Petit os vif près de l'automne
Petit os vif près du chant.

Remue couleur de Saturne
L'adieu d'oiseaux bruns.

The Woman Taciturn

Await Saturn's color
Which constructs and instructs
In your time.
On the brown lintel among your trunks of stone
Banqueting
Under the mantelet
The winter the feed of next winter
The same and the same time.

Fastidious incantatress
Binding leaf and feather
In your woodland workshop
Woman with taciturn treasures.

It is your only joy when your fingers
Are raised out toward the setting sun
The clavicle of the wood thrush
Bare little bone near the autumn
Bare little bone near the song.

Stirring Saturn's color
The farewells of brown birds.

La Belle Au Bois Dormant

Que me devais-tu de ce pourpoint rose
Quand j'aimais encore respirer
Au bout du temps entre les piliers des ormes du lit.
Tu as traîné dans la forêt toutes tes branches
J'écoutais ton sang dans tes cheveux doux
J'écoutais le vent à des milliers d'années.

Sleeping Beauty

How you owed me for this pink pourpoint
When I still loved to breathe
At the end of time between the bed's elm pillars.
In the forest you dragged all your branches
I listened to your blood within your soft hair
I listened to the wind thousands of years passed.

Miracle

Orion se lève
Chasse au pré le lièvre
Puis une qui sauve
L'animal virant
Au pied des tribus
Isis le tolère.

D'abord des tintements puis levées dans l'espace
Les deux bleues qui riaient maîtresse et la servante.

On ne se confiera qu'à la vierge Marie
Tourneuse de soleils. Sous elle à la Brodée
Qui va les bras ballants sur le quai des prairies
Au voyage des eaux des filets et des pies.

Honore la mère de dieu
Et toute bête qu'elle tient
Les yeux de l'oiseau voient ses mains.

Le lièvre parcourt
La rosée d'aurore
Au pré dentelé
O chaires des bois
Vieux pèlerinages
Durement quittés.

À présent la pierre
Le diamant gris
C'est aux cathédrales
Lunes de midi
Plus belles dehors.

Miracle

Orion rises
Hunts hare in the meadow
Then one who saves
The animal veering
At the foot of the tribes.
This Isis tolerates.

First ringing then lifted into space
The two blues laugh mistress and servant.

We will only confide in the virgin Mary
Spinner of suns. Under her in the embroidered
Which goes arms dangling over the quay of the prairies
On the journey of waters and nets and magpies.

Honor the mother of god
And every beast she keeps
Bird eyes watch her hands.

The hare crosses
Aurora's dews
In the perforated meadow
O wooden pulpits
Old pilgrimages
Dourly abandoned.

Now the stone
The grey diamond
It is with cathedrals
Midday moons
Most beautiful outside.

Venus Mercure Jupiter. Les nuages passent.

Un bras rond chargé de cœurs ouvre le faîte
Le toit le dos du ciel je ne sais quel.
Au zénith certain
D'un côté de l'autre
Dans le même instant
Sans me diriger

J'ai vu tes deux draps
Noués le vert le rose
En haut des dessus
Éternellement.

Honore la mère de dieu
L'air de partout sur ses genoux.

Chartres, 1975

Venus Mercury Jupiter. Clouds pass.

A round arm full of hearts parts the ridge
The roof the back of the sky I don't know which
In the certain zenith
From one side to the other
In a single instant
Without guidance

I saw your two cloths
Tying the green and pink
At the summit of summits
Eternally.

Honor the mother of god
The air of everywhere upon her knees.

Chartres, 1975

Lovers Elona and Rubia embrace in the shady jungles of Chandannagar.
Collage illustration by Valentine Penrose.
Dons des féminines (Librarie Les Pas perdus, 1951).

Translator's Note: The Saturnine Sorcery of Valentine Penrose

Mia X. Pérez

> *[What kind of hope do you place in love?] No hope: the pronouncement of an irremediable malady, that of always having to distinguish, according to life, between I the subject and you the object.*[1]
>
> —Valentine Penrose

Valentine Penrose's engagement with the arcane was particular in its breadth, depth, and practice. Enrolling in the Sorbonne to study Eastern philosophy and later living in Indian ashrams, her understanding of spirituality soared far beyond an academic interest in, say, alchemy or Kabbalah in Western Europe. Her constant use of divinatory systems of no specific denomination, as well as her profound, perhaps even obliterating, identification with nature and the nonhuman were foundational to her sensibilities as a poet and as a woman. While occult imagery, ubiquitous in the works of early surrealists, was often viewed as yet another face of the taboo to liberate and unleash, for Penrose esotericism, magic, and the occult were lived practices that influenced her work not only aesthetically but experientially and politically. Her commitment to authentic spiritual transcendence, compounded by her supposed tendency toward rigidity and stubbornness, did not align well with the urban, modern surrealist project. Yet, she remained steadfast in her mystical rebellion, even throughout her divorce from Roland Penrose, in which her monastic temperament is thought to have been one of the decisive factors.

Penrose's ethereal mysticism and beauty allowed others to perceive her as an enchanting muse with second sight. To those close to her, it seemed that she had a capacity for magic and divination that enveloped everything and everyone around her. Her natural comportment while navigating the world appeared to reveal the extraordinary within the most mundane levels of life. Her aptitude for clairvoyance was so strong that it purportedly terrified Antony Penrose, the then young son of Lee Miller and Roland Penrose whom she would care for during her stays at Farley Farm. Though the strength of her powers were intimidating, Antony was nonetheless comforted by her air of protection and safety. He recalls how, rain or shine, she would take long, meandering walks through the property's expansive woods and never fail to return with some magical object in her hand such as a "bulk of knotted wood, a dried mushroom, or even a mummified toad. Occasionally, she brought back rare plants which she secretly planted in the garden."[2] Similarly, Hélène Azenor, painter and lover of Penrose, believed the elusive poet could conjure strange and uncanny scenes that defied common sense:

> Further on, at the end of a court, she discovered a factory of automatons whose fixed expressions we distinguished through the dust-covered windows. Again, I was drawn into a magical universe beyond normal life, and I was starving for it. When that universe withdrew from me, I lost everything, even a basic sense of the beyond. Didn't I know that a spell is not forever. And, when I was disenchanted, delivered from its power, I fell back into everyday life, the life of everyone else. How not to believe it was for my pleasure that she created these bizarre locations through love. That it was for my greatest joy she had led me to discover one after the other . . .

> Proving that everything was magical with her, when I wished by myself to see what she had caused me to love, I found nothing . . . And, in those moments when I searched for all that had been loved and relished, I heard her voice: "Hélène, I love you, it's true, my little page, my love is deep!"[3]

Irrespective of the possibilities or impossibilities of the proposed scenario, Penrose's love for and attentiveness to the world around her was so singular that she became Delphic in the eyes of her companions, causing them to question the very limits of physical reality. Everywhere she went, Penrose seemed to effortlessly realize the prophetic surrealist *elsewhere*.

Derived from André Breton's proclamation in the *Surrealist Manifesto* that "existence is elsewhere," the *elsewhere* of surrealism gestures toward an oneiric realm of uninhibited imagination and desire that is activated through the production and consumption of surrealist art. Penrose, however, was less interested in the psychoanalytic effects of her work. Her poems do not read like dreams or fantasies in the strictest sense. They read rather like ouroboric incantations. Throughout her oeuvre, the surrealist technique of automatism returns to its origins in the spiritualist movement and the Romantics who preceded them, and the medium of art becomes one with the practice of mediumship itself. My translations of Penrose's work were born from this problem: How does one translate language that not only pushes itself beyond the bounds of narrative logic but is written from, with, and for a supernatural impetus? How does one translate a spell?

Casting a spell, though sometimes maintaining a semantic relation to its end goal as one might see in the contemporary practice of positive affirmations, is often as simple as singing an elongated vowel, humming a single note, or uttering a symbolic phrase that is believed to be "charged" by its own enunciation. During my own years as a young dilettantish acolyte flittering between various meditation chambers and ritual temples in Seattle, WA, I repeatedly observed how speech transformed spatial and subjective experience. Spending thirty to forty-five minutes incessantly chanting inevitably results in a palpable physical shift in one's perceptual, sensorial, and emotional awareness. It activates all senses in the body while at the same time promoting intense relaxation. Because of its capacity to alter states of mind (whatever the nature of that alteration may be), vocalization and spell work has for millennia been used as the magical means by which alternate realms are opened and closed, entities invoked and banished.

In many ways, literary translation itself can be an invocation, an opening up of oneself and one's tongue to call in and upon another. It is itself a means of enchanting and becoming enchanted. By reading these poems as spells, formed out of a shapeshifting language which Paul Éluard describes as "the forgetting, the magic screen, before which, every color, every nuance, every idea is new," Penrose's capacity for conjuring novel unseen worlds becomes abundantly clear. Penrose's words had to be approached from a mystical point of view.

For this reason, Penrose's most recurrent symbols, including but not limited to mirrors, surfaces, water, circles, minerals, medicinal herbs, caverns, birds, weaving, and mythical creatures, as well as her incessant trains of discrepant if not contradictory prepositional phrases ("the green father and mother/of pledges of voice of wings and of silk/lady of all up above in her joy"), can be interpreted as her unique rendering of religious and spiritual concepts. The constant unfolding and fractalization of images resonate with philosophical principles such as Maya, the illusory dualism that conceals the nature of reality in Buddhism and Hinduism, as well as those of the Great Work and Grail Quest of medieval European traditions. It is important to note, though, that Penrose's poems overflow with allegory, myth, and spiritual dialogue without ever sacrificing her incantatory rhythm. Not infrequently, Penrose's lines appear entirely disarticulated, and proceed from a nonfigurative source beyond symbolism, making them noncompliant with standard grammatical sense-making. Genders, tenses, and pronouns alter the poem's significance in ways that English cannot always accommodate. In instances where there is truly no English equivalent (for example, "je suis vivant, je suis vivante"), the formal and sonic qualities are instead foregrounded ("I am alive, I am a life").

It is also worth noting that Penrose herself experimented with literary translation. Notes for a translation of Jean Rhys' novel *Wide Sargasso Sea*, also adapted in this collection as "Madwoman of Sargassum," is archived in the Roland Penrose collection at the National Galleries of Scotland. Interestingly, poems occasionally include non-French phrases or words that Penrose decidedly did not translate, and those phrases remain untranslated here. There is one case, though, that warrants examining in greater detail.

Appearing in the ultimate line of "[Dear to love you like an awakening daisy]," *niranes* is not a French, Spanish, or English term and has for the duration of my work on this project remained a bit of an etymological mystery. While the possibility of a typo in the original work is entirely feasible (*nirane* is quite close to the French *narine* for nostril), it is just as likely that Penrose was utilizing a term, or more precisely a transliteration of a term, from a language historically understudied by anglo- and francophones. Considering her transnational temperament and her study of Sanskrit, it is worth thinking outside of the box here. In Arabic, the word نَار (nar) translates to "fire" or "flame" with نِيرَان (niran) being the plural form of the noun. In Sanskrit, नीर (nira) translates to "water" and नीरद (nirada) to "cloud" or, literally, "water-giver." While neither term exactly matches Penrose's *niranes*, it opens a wealth of poetic imagery that is already greatly aligned with the poet's core sensibilities. Furthermore, reading the line in its entirety as it describes a figure "pomponné [dolled up, dressed up] de niranes d'étoiles noires [black stars] et de galanes [either penstemon or chelone flowers]," there is a poetic resonance between the *pompon* (literally pompom or bobble) of *pomponné*, the black stars, and the bright flowers and the images of fires or clouds or even both simultaneously. For this reason, *niranes* remains an opening in the translation that transcends the poem itself. Even if it is a typo, it is worth embracing—in the true Surrealist fashion—as an expression of chance. Thus, *niranes* is perhaps best read as a glitch through which distant and ancient poetry may be glimpsed.

The collisions of past and present as well as of the here and the elsewhere, the evocations of fairy tales and myths, the rapturous sensorial-imaginative freefalls which populate these poems may not be unfamiliar to readers of eighteenth- and nineteenth-century Romantic, Gothic, and Symbolist literature. These poems, in their anarchic spiritualism, their spatial and subjective self-displacement, break the bounds of time to coalesce literary and religious history into their own expansive mythos. And yet, there is undoubtedly a melancholic and antimodern signature to this displacement that disjoints Penrose from her Surrealist milieu and aligns her more intimately with the writers of centuries past. In addition, then, to synthesizing religious and occult symbolism from Catholicism, Hinduism, alchemy, tarot, astrology, Vedic philosophy, Gnosticism, British "paganism," Egyptian cosmology, and more, Penrose's poems are full of conspicuous intertextual allusions to literary legends such as Charles Perrault, François-René de Chateaubriand, Alphonse de Lamartine, Antoine Galland, Arthur Rimbaud, and even anglophone Romantics like Percy Bysshe Shelley, Ann Radcliffe, William Blake, the Brontës, and Edgar Allan Poe. As is the case with many of these authors, the body, the natural world, and the constructs of civilization are triangulated as sites of ontological, affective, and metaphysical instability that house experiences of both spiritual liberation and abjection. To quote Antony Penrose once more, "the planes of place and time held no firm attachment for [Valentine]. She was a spirit woman, not wholly present or comfortable in the exquisite body she had chosen for her stay in this world."[4]

To read these poems, one must surrender entirely to the resonance of the image and abandon all concern regarding subject-object or space-time differentiation. Penrose's adoption of the collage is as important as her use of automatism, not only in the construction of an image or sequence of images but in the destruction of the borders between subject and object. In some poems, one may encounter a stable lyrical "I" speaking to the beloved in a chivalric mood. In many others, though, the "I" that presumably addressed the object quickly dissolves into the landscape, and the "you" that presumably represented the beloved has transformed into a divine entity, a place, a plant, or an unnamed element of being that has spontaneously formed within the poem's cuts and creases. In still others, "I" the subject and "you" the object are forever in flux; while they are doomed to remain separated, as Penrose states, "according to life," the collaged landscapes of bodies and bugs, deserts and mirrors, shadows and glimmers, grant a glimpse of the eco-erotic loss of the individual in all its queer Romantic splendor.

Consider, for example, a poem such as "For a Woman For a Road," in which the figures and their landscape transform at an unparalleled pace. The title alone proposes a complex ambiguity since it is uncertain whether the woman and the road are two separate figures or if the woman, potentially presenting the poet with the possibility of journey, is a sort of road in herself. The ambiguity, however, is exponentially heightened within the body of the poem. Two feminine bodies are introduced, each qualified with its own respective "here" which indicates that the bodies are not eternally or essentially feminine but undergoing a transient feminine form.

With two bodies immediately in the mix, the pronoun introduced in the seventh line could easily indicate either figure. Originally the relative neuter pronoun *qui*, the translation to "she" is intended to clarify the stark femininity of the figures as bodies dissolve into the scenery rather than to subjectivize any one figure over the other.

> This body here feminine hangs like a
>   distant droplet
> toward the other here feminine this time
> where hair even across the smile
>   mad spindle
>   sharpened bones
> she will cross plains with her hips
> she will beat the straw not the swaddle she will
>   sleep
>   in the granges
> alone for the herbs
> for whom the friend will never worry however green

The poem continues by fluctuating quickly between the use of third person and the use of first and second person. The endearing address to "my brown mouse" transitions suddenly to the cryptic but nonetheless violent image of the feminine body being "seized by breasts by hands by hair / never released entirely herself," before returning once more to an intimacy of mutual recognition and construction in the last line of the third stanza: "by all the ends urgent false / I spun you you wove me." The two figures seem to simultaneously inhabit the roles of forbidden lovers, natural forces, and even, perhaps, alienated perspectives of a single subject. Instead of attempting to derive a coherent narrative from a poem in which it does not exist, the translation must prioritize the poem's disintegration, dynamic landscapes, and affective contortionism.

Walter Benjamin's conceptions of ruin, translation, and language have greatly informed my approach here. I see in these poems what Benjamin calls the tragic aesthetic of "irresistible decay" wherein "events of history shrivel up and become absorbed in the setting."[5] It follows that the poem's absorption of what has passed reflects nature's orientation toward decay by way of its overwhelming ripeness, its "after-ripeness."[6] The abundant eco-collages of Penrose's oeuvre thus function funereally, sacrificially, and phantasmically as they demonstrate the painful fact of discontinuity while asserting their own magical potential as spells to overcome it. In this way, my translation attempts to capture Penrose's saturnine sorcery through its own ruinous process. As Derrida speculates in his essay on relevant translation, "Translation is devoted to ruin, to that form of memory or commemoration that is called a ruin; ruin is perhaps its vocation and a destiny that it accepts it from the very outset."[7]

Until this collection, the poetry of Valentine Penrose has been virtually inaccessible both in the United States and France with the exception of a now rare 1977 edition titled *Poems and Narrations*, a bilingual selection of prose and poetic works translated by British painter and Farley Farm resident Roy Edwards. Organized by Roland as a sort of parting gift to Valentine while her health deteriorated from cancer, the collection acknowledges and attributes much to Penrose's Gothic, Romantic, and mystical influences. Edwards, a queer artist himself, uses his translation to lean into Penrose's already unapologetic sapphic eroticism and feminine worship. However, despite introducing the collection as "hermetic," the translations do little to relay the work's mystical, ephemeral elements and their intrinsic connection to the sexual and gendered motifs so crucial to her gaze. Arriving nearly fifty years after Edwards's translation and one hundred years after Valentine Penrose's first publication in *Les Cahiers du Sud*, this book brings together all poems from *Imagerie d'Épinal*,

Herbe à la lune, *Poèmes*, *Sorts de la lueur,* and *Les Magies,* as well as the uncollected poems that were published in the literary magazines *DYN*, *Fulcrum*, and *Cahiers d'Arts*, and those first published in *Poems and Narrations* such as "For Paul," "Tomb for Marie-Berthe," "The Woman Taciturn," "Sleeping Beauty," and "Miracle."

I can only hope that this translation substantiates the legacy of this mercurial poet and benevolent sorceress who habitually snuck out of her desolate chateau to bask nude in the forest moonlight amongst the nocturnal wild ones.[8]

Notes

1 Valentine Penrose, "Enquête sur l'amour," in *La Revolution Surréaliste*, no. 12 (Dec 1929).

2 Antony Penrose, "Préface," in *Écrits d'une femme surréaliste* (Paris: Joelle Losfeld, 2001), 7–8.

3 Hélène Azénor, *Vivre Tout Haut* (Paris: Les Octariennes, 1989), 205–7, quoted in Penrose, Écrits, 282.

4 Antony Penrose, *The Friendly Surrealist* (Munich: Prestel Verlag, 2001), 28.

5 Walter Benjamin, *The Origin of German Tragic Drama* (London: New Left Books, 1977), 179–182.

6 Walter Benjamin, "The Translator's Task," *TTR* 10, no. 2 (1997): 155.

7 Jacques Derrida, "What is a 'Relevant' Translation?" in *The Translation Studies Reader*, ed. Lawrence Venuti (New York: Routledge, 2021), 378–9.

8 Antony Penrose, *The Friendly Surrealist* (Munich: Prestel Verlag, 2001), 59.

Cock Norah appears, winning Rubia's loveless hand in a duel.
Collage illustration by Valentine Penrose.
Dons des féminines (Librarie Les Pas perdus, 1951).

Translator's Acknowledgments

Firstly, Matvei Yankelevich and World Poetry Books receive my endless gratitude for believing in this project and maintaining the persistence and patience necessary to realize it. Many thanks to Ilan Erikson Weisbrod, Anne Osherson, Julia Kiernan, Henry Gifford, and Roz Shayan Naimi whose meaningful comments and insights made this publication possible, and especially to Chris Clarke whose meticulous close readings and formal suggestions can be felt throughout these pages.

I'd also like to thank the friends and colleagues who supported this undertaking through conversation and workshop with special appreciation to Jennifer Grotz and our Bread Loaf cohort who never hesitated to ask the difficult (and most important) questions.

I'm also grateful to Black Sun Lit editor and dear friend Jared Daniel Fagen for publishing early versions of these poems as well as to the editors at *Tupelo Quarterly*, *California Quarterly*, and *mercury firs* who have published excerpts from this collection.

Lastly, I'm forever thankful to Don, our tabbies, and all other creatures who continue to carry the fire. This translation is dedicated to A and B.

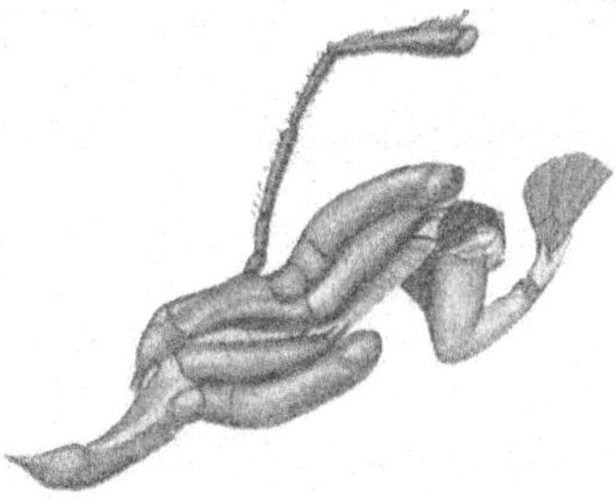

Valentine Penrose, at Pouy, Hautes-Pyrénées, south-western France, ca. 1935.
Photographer unknown.

Valentine Penrose (1898–1978) was born in Mont-de-Marsan, France to a bourgeois military family. Disinterested in conforming to any social convention, Penrose immersed herself in bohemian circles from a young age. Commonly celebrated as the first woman to publish Surrealist poetry, Penrose's poems are distinguished by their intertextuality and anachronism, shaped by her lifelong studies in eastern philosophies, medieval history, and magical practice. Restless in the tame suburbs of France and England, she frequently traveled abroad, with long stays in India. She joined the international brigades in the Spanish Civil War and was stationed with French forces in Algiers during WWII. Perhaps best known for the unapologetically queer 1951 gothic novel *The Bloody Countess*, Penrose authored several works of poetry, prose, and collage before passing away on Farley Farm, the artist commune run by ex-husband Roland Penrose and his second wife Lee Miller.

Mia X. Pérez is a writer, editor, and translator from Seattle, Washington. Their work has been published in *The Brooklyn Review*, *Milk Press*, *AGON*, *Black Sun Lit*, among others. Currently a PhD candidate of Comparative Literature at The Graduate Center, CUNY, their research focuses on Romanticism, ecological thought, and the aesthetics of decay. Valentine Penrose's complete poems, *Of Thorn and Wing*, is their first book of translation.

Felicity Gee is the author of *Magic Realism, World Cinema, and the Avant-Garde* (Routledge) and has published extensively on surrealism, women artists, film and affect theory, including essays on Raúl Ruiz, Leonora Carrington, Claude Cahun, Jean Cocteau, Kōbō Abe, Angela Carter, and Fredric Jameson. She edited the scholarly volume *Valentine Penrose: Surrealist, Poet, Artist, Voyager* (Bloomsbury). From 2023 to 2025, Gee was President of the International Society for the Study of Surrealism, and currently serves on the editorial board of the *International Journal of Surrealism*. She is Associate Professor of Modernist Literatures and Avant-Garde Studies at the University of Exeter and her current project is a comparative study of women artists and writers of the modernist period and the architectural body.

This book was typeset in PS Fournier, a transitional serif inspired by the eighteenth-century romans of Pierre-Simon Fournier. It was designed by Stéphane Elbaz for Typofonderie, Paris. The cover, designed by Andrew Bourne at Clever Hans, is based on archival portraits of Valentine Penrose and emulates solarization—a darkroom technique associated with Surrealism, most famously employed by Man Ray and Lee Miller. The interior features decorative elements and collage illustrations done by Valentine Penrose for the 1951 book *Dons des féminines*. Typesetting by Don't Look Now. Printed and bound in Lithuania by BALTO Print. Manufactured by Arctic Paper in Sweden, the paper in this book meets EU Ecolabel, Forest Stewardship Council, and Cradle to Cradle certification standards.

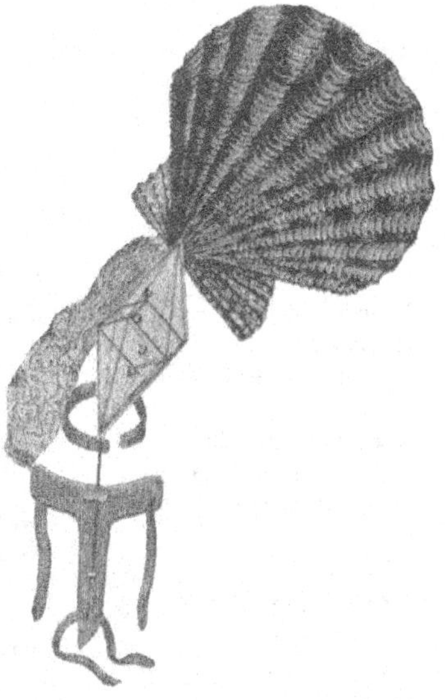

WORLD POETRY

Samer Abu Hawwash
Ruins and Other Poems
tr. Huda J. Fakhreddine

Marie-Noëlle Agniau
The Escapades
tr. Jesse Hover Amar

Nadia Anjuman
Smoke Drifts
tr. Diana Arterian
& Marina Omar

Jean-Paul Auxeméry
Selected Poems
tr. Nathaniel Tarn

Leire Bilbao
Between Fish Scales
tr. Joana Urtasun

Boethius
The Poems from On the Consolation of Philosophy
tr. Peter Glassgold

Maria Borio
Transparencies
tr. Danielle Pieratti

Astrid Cabral
Spotlight on the Word
tr. Alexis Levitin

Jeannette L. Clariond
Goddesses of Water
tr. Samantha Schnee

Jacques Darras
John Scotus Eriugena at Laon
tr. Richard Sieburth

Mario dell'Arco
Day Lasts Forever
tr. Marc Alan Di Martino
JOSEPH TUSIANI ITALIAN TRANSLATION PRIZE

Marie de Quatrebarbes
The Vitals
tr. Aiden Farrell

Ricardo Domeneck
First Epistle to the Amphibians
tr. Chris Daniels

Dordzhi Dzhaldzhireev
Beyond Salvation
tr. Venya Gushchin

Olivia Elias
Chaos, Crossing
tr. Kareem James Abu-Zeid

Gastón Fernández
Apparent Breviary
tr. KM Cascia

Jerzy Ficowski
Everything I Don't Know
tr. Jennifer Grotz
& Piotr Sommer
PEN AWARD FOR POETRY IN TRANSLATION

Antonio Gamoneda
Book of the Cold
tr. Katherine M. Hedeen &
Víctor Rodríguez Núñez

Mireille Gansel
Soul House
tr. Joan Seliger Sidney

Óscar García Sierra
Houston, I'm the problem
tr. Carmen Yus Quintero

Phoebe Giannisi
Homerica
tr. Brian Sneeden

Zuzanna Ginczanka
On Centaurs & Other Poems
tr. Alex Braslavsky

Julien Gracq
Abounding Freedom
tr. Alice Yang

Tonino Guerra
The Honey
tr. Nathan Dunne

Ernst Herbeck
In His One Languages
tr. Gary Sullivan &
David Brazil

Karmelo C. Iribarren
You've Heard This One Before
tr. John R. Sesgo

Leeladhar Jagoori
What of the Earth Was Saved
tr. Matt Reeck

Nakedness Is My End: Poems from the Greek Anthology
tr. Edmund Keeley

Birhan Keskin
Earthly Conditions
tr. Öykü Tekten

Mohammed Khaïr-Eddine
Quasars
tr. Jake Syersak

Jazra Khaleed
The Light That Burns Us
ed. Karen Van Dyck

Judith Kiros
O
tr. Kira Josefsson

Dimitra Kotoula
The Slow Horizon That Breathes
tr. Maria Nazos

Dmitry Kuzmin
Legit Target
ed. Polina Barskova
& Kevin M. F. Platt

Maria Laina
Hers
tr. Karen Van Dyck

Maria Laina
Rose Fear
tr. Sarah McCann

Perrin Langda
A Few Microseconds on Earth
tr. Pauline Levy Valensi

Anna Malihon
Girl with a Bullet
tr. Olena Jennings

Afrizal Malna
Document Shredding Museum
tr. Daniel Owen
NATIONAL TRANSLATION AWARD

Joyce Mansour
In the Glittering Maw
tr. C. Francis Fisher

Manuel Maples Arce
Stridentist Poems
tr. KM Cascia

Vlado Martek
Pre-Poetry
ed. Branislav Jakovljević
tr. Ainsley Morse

Selma Meerbaum-Eisinger
Song of the Yellow Asters
tr. Carlie Hoffman

Ennio Moltedo
New Things
tr. Marguerite Feitlowitz

Ennio Moltedo
Night
tr. Marguerite Feitlowitz

Meret Oppenheim
The Loveliest Vowel Empties
tr. Kathleen Heil

Nicanor Parra
The Christ of Elqui Poems
tr. KM Cascia

Giovanni Pascoli
Last Dream
tr. Geoffrey Brock
RAIZISS/DE PALCHI TRANSLATION AWARD

Valentine Penrose
Of Thorn and Wing
tr. Mia X. Pérez

Gabriel Pomerand
Saint Ghetto of the Loans
tr. Michael Kasper & Bhamati Viswanathan

Liliana Ponce
Theory of the Voice and Dream
tr. Michael Martin Shea
PEN AWARD FOR POETRY IN TRANSLATION

Rainer Maria Rilke
Where the Paths Do Not Go
tr. Burton Pike

Amelia Rosselli
Document
tr. Roberta Antognini & Deborah Woodard

Elisabeth Rynell
Night Talks
tr. Rika Lesser

Waly Salomão
Border Fare
tr. Maryam Monalisa Gharavi

George Sarantaris
Abyss and Song
tr. Pria Louka

Yan Satunovsky
Prosthetics Factory
tr. Ainsley Morse & Philip Redko

George Seferis
Book of Exercises II
tr. Jennifer R. Kellogg
ELIZABETH CONSTANTINIDES MEMORIAL TRANSLATION PRIZE

Seo Jung Hak
The Cheapest France in Town
tr. Megan Sungyoon

Ahmad Shamlou
Elegies of the Earth
tr. Niloufar Talebi
HAROLD MORTON LANDON TRANSLATION AWARD

Dan Sociu
Deep Fakes
tr. Monica Cure

Edith Södergran
Modern Woman
tr. CD Eskilson

Ardengo Soffici
Simultaneities & Lyric Chemisms
tr. Olivia E. Sears

Liesl Ujvary
Good & Safe
tr. Ann Cotten & Anna-Isabella Dinwoodie

Paul Verlaine
Before Wisdom: The Early Poems
tr. Keith Waldrop & K.A. Hays

Haris Vlavianos
Renaissance
tr. Patricia Felisa Barbeito

Witold Wirpsza
Apotheosis of Music
tr. Frank L. Vigoda

Uljana Wolf
kochanie, today i bought bread
tr. Greg Nissan

Ye Lijun
My Mountain Country
tr. Fiona Sze-Lorrain

Verónica Zondek
Cold Fire
tr. Katherine Silver